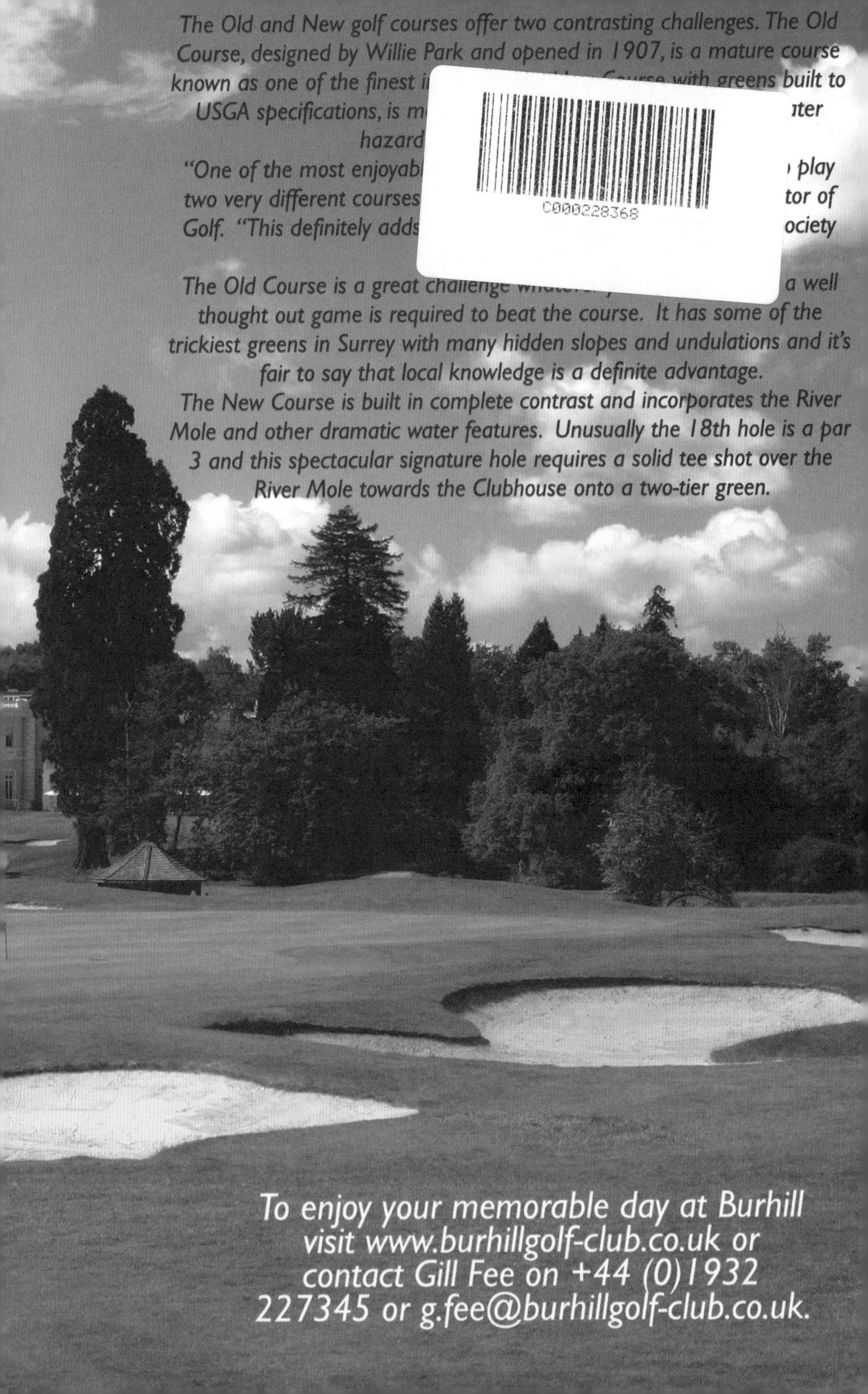

The Old and New golf courses offer two contrasting challenges. The Old Course, designed by Willie Park and opened in 1907, is a mature course known as one of the finest i ... with greens built to USGA specifications, is m ... ater hazard
"One of the most enjoyab ... play two very different courses ... tor of Golf. "This definitely adds ... ociety
The Old Course is a great challenge ... a well thought out game is required to beat the course. It has some of the trickiest greens in Surrey with many hidden slopes and undulations and it's fair to say that local knowledge is a definite advantage.
The New Course is built in complete contrast and incorporates the River Mole and other dramatic water features. Unusually the 18th hole is a par 3 and this spectacular signature hole requires a solid tee shot over the River Mole towards the Clubhouse onto a two-tier green.
To enjoy your memorable day at Burhill visit www.burhillgolf-club.co.uk or contact Gill Fee on +44 (0)1932 227345 or g.fee@burhillgolf-club.co.uk.

Top 100 Golf Courses of England

2007 - 2008

Walton Heath Golf Club (Old Course)

Top 100 Golf Courses of England

2007 - 2008

Wentworth Club (Edinburgh Course)

Keith Baxter

Top 100 Golf Courses Of England 2007 – 2008

Keith Baxter

June 2007

Graphic design by Nick Oliver.
Course descriptions by Keith Baxter and Andy Newmarch except Delamere Forest by John Mulder.
Photography by Top 100 Golf Courses except where stated.

ISBN 978-0-9554956-1-8

Published by Top 100 Golf Courses Limited
Stone Farm, Bere Ferrers, Devon, PL20 7JY
www.top100golfcourses.co.uk

Printed in Hong Kong

Uncaptioned photographs
Front cover — Prince's (Kevin Murray), back cover — Worplesdon (Andy Taylor)

Mannings Heath Golf Club - Waterfall Course

Contents

The Top 100 Golf Courses of England

Acknowledgements

The views in this book are the combined and rounded opinions of dozens of club professionals, golf course architects, club officials and thousands of passionate golfers. We are genuinely grateful that so many people visit the Top 100 website (www.top100golfcourses.co.uk) every day and are especially indebted to those who take the time to post passionate course reviews, hundreds of which are included in this book.

The quality of the photographs we receive via email every day is quite stunning and we are grateful to those who have allowed us to print their remarkable images. This book would not have been possible without their input.

Thanks must also go to the many golf club officials, too numerous to mention by name. We are touched by their kind words, generous support and for allowing us to play and photograph their stunning golf courses.

We also acknowledge the golf magazines and their teams of panellists who take the business of ranking golf courses as seriously as we do.

It's impossible for us to name everyone who has helped us, but we would especially like to mention: Stewart Abramson, Paul Edwards, Cédric Hannedouche, Jim McCann, Kevin Murray, Alex Sherratt, Andy Taylor and Rod Wiltshire.

Special thanks go to our close friends and family whose patience has been well and truly tried.

Aldeburgh Golf Club

Golf in England

England was formed as a country in the 10th century following Anglo Saxon invasions in the 5th and 6th centuries when marauding tribes of warriors from the Netherlands, Germany and Denmark bravely crossed the North Sea in wooden rowing boats in search of fertile farmlands. The Anglo Saxons slowly began to take control but they failed to conquer Cornwall and Offa's Dyke kept them out of Wales. Naturally, Scotland was a total no-go area for Saxons because fierce Scottish tribes kept the invaders at bay from the northern side of Hadrian's Wall.

It's unclear when golf in England was first played but it is likely that the game started to spread southwards from Scotland after the Treaty of Glasgow was signed in 1501 and a truce was declared between Henry VII of England and James IV of Scotland. The earliest documented evidence is contained in a letter written in 1513 by Queen Catherine of England (Catherine Parr), sixth wife of Henry VIII. In her letter to Cardinal Wolsey, she refers to the growing popularity of golf in England.

When the unmarried Queen Elizabeth I of England died in 1603, James VI of Scotland moved court to London, becoming James I of England and taking up residence at the Royal Palace in Greenwich. His royal entourage is thought to have contained a number of golfers and they found the perfect ground at Blackheath on which to play their beloved game. In 1608, Blackheath Golf Club was instituted, but documentary evidence has yet to be discovered.

According to Royal Blackheath Golf Club, "the Club's own artefacts evidence its existence as early as 1745, and the Edinburgh Almanac – which has listed the dates of formation of the leading golfing societies since the early 1800s – records Blackheath as having been established "prior to 1745", as far back as 1830. Our claim to be the world's oldest golf club has thus remained unchallenged for over 175 years." Blackheath Golf Club was officially founded in 1766.

"Now I come to the course of the Royal Blackheath Golf Club, the premier golf club of the world," wrote Bernard Darwin in ***The Golf Courses of Great Britain***, "and I come to it with a heavy heart because this historic club plays no longer on its historic heath. Hordes of vandal boys playing football have kicked the sacred turf to pieces and made golf impossible. The holes are no longer cut and the club has moved to Eltham. The Eltham course is in a pretty, park-like spot with admiral greens and a fine old club-house, but it is of course not the heath." Founded in 1864, Royal North Devon at Westward Ho! is the oldest course in England still playing along its original fairways and since these early beginnings, golf in England has exploded.

Today there are more than 740,000 golfers affiliated to England's 1,900 or so golf clubs. There are more golf courses in England than Ireland, Scotland and Wales put together. The topographical variation of England's golf courses is perhaps totally unique the world over. There's an unusual maritime strip of heathland, which has been home to Aldebugh Golf Club for approaching 125 years. Since 1891, the wonderful clifftop course at Sheringham Golf Club has entertained generations of golfers, but sadly it narrowly missed our current English Top 100. The sandbelt to the west of London was where heathland golf started with the foundation of Woking Golf Club in 1893. Other clubs soon blossomed as they laid their courses out on this light, free draining soil, the majority of which seem to have the letter "W" at the beginning of their name! Sandy moorland ground ensures crisp turf at Moortown and Bovey Castle, whereas majestic, ancient parkland can be found at Little Aston and Stoke Park. Modern American-styled tournament layouts meld with old parkland at The Belfry and Forest of Arden, whereas the exquisite Duchess course at Woburn is carved through a pine forest.

Naturally, it's the seaside links courses which provide the magnetic attraction for the vast majority of travelling golfers, especially those courses with an Open Championship pedigree. The course on the front cover is the only non-royal Open Championship commoner in England. Prince's has played host to only one Open and that was back in 1932, so it has perhaps slipped the memories of most. We are delighted to bring this unsung gem into the limelight and we hope that you enjoy reading about not only the English household names, but also England's lesser-known courses.

Happy reading, but more importantly, play well.

Keith Baxter

The Top 100 Ranking, Rating and Review Systems

Rankings

1st to **100th** or in some cases **125th** or more

First of all, we acknowledge that many golf magazines do a great biennial job of ranking our greatest golf courses and long may they continue to do so. However, our process is unique and many have told us that we actually do it better than the magazines themselves.

With input from a statistician at Cambridge University, we built a comprehensive database that contains historical ranking information from golf magazines and other publications. Then we applied a series of rules and weightings favouring the world rankings, the most recent rankings and the frequency that courses appear on ranking lists. This process has, in effect, created our unique ranking for each course and it is perhaps best described as the consensus of consensuses, which we can drill down to country level.

Naturally, ranking golf courses is not an objective process in the first place, but we feel that nobody does it better. And, to add our own dimension, we factor in our own Top 100 ranking, generated by course review ratings posted on the Top 100 website (www.top100golfcourses.co.uk) by passionate golfers from all walks of life.

Ratings

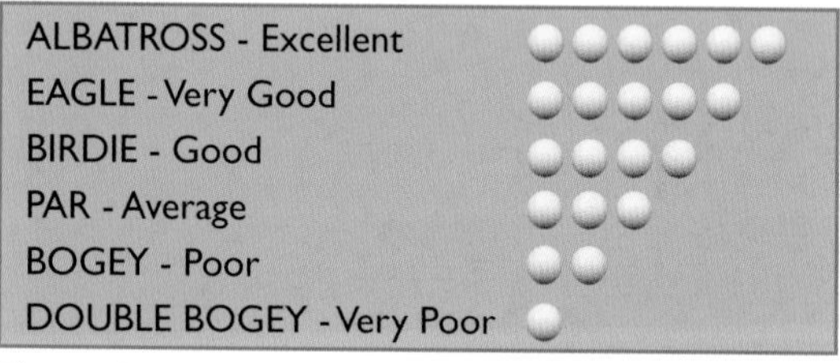

ALBATROSS - Excellent
EAGLE - Very Good
BIRDIE - Good
PAR - Average
BOGEY - Poor
DOUBLE BOGEY - Very Poor

The main part of the Top 100 website course review process requires the course reviewer to rate the course for which they are writing a review. We decided to make the rating system simple and set no specific rules for rating a golf course except, naturally, that the reviewer should have played it. Important factors, such as course design, condition, difficulty, variety and historical importance are all left for the reviewer to judge.

Each course can only receive one rating for each posted review. Rather than using a star rating system, we decided to use a golf ball rating. If, for example, reviewer a) decides to give Royal Birkdale a four-ball rating and reviewer b) gives Birkdale a six-ball rating, then Birkdale will show five balls. However, if reviewer a) gives Birkdale a five-ball rating and reviewer b) gives Birkdale six balls, then Birkdale will show five and a half balls. The Top 100 website automatically calculates the number of golf balls allocated to each course by averaging the reviewers' ratings and then we have a rounding up process implemented to the nearest half or full ball.

We took a snapshot of the website's reviewers' golf ball ratings for each course in December 2006 and the golf ball rating is shown on each course page in this book but you'll need to see the website for the absolute latest position.

Once again we have created our own Top 100 list based on the golf ball rating system (see page 218) and we've factored these statistics into our comprehensive ranking database.

Reviewers' Comments

All the comments on the left hand pages (even numbers) are edited extracts from reviews posted on the Top 100 website by passionate golfers. Anybody can write a course review and, since we published our first book in June 2005, more than 2,000 new course reviews have been written and posted online by all types of golfer from the professional to the high handicapper. We think these honest comments really cut to the chase and bring this book and the Top 100 website to life.

If you want to influence the Top 100 rankings and have something to say about the Top 100 courses you've played, then visit the website at www.top100golfcourses.co.uk and write a course review. If you agree or disagree with any of the course reviews posted online then you have the right to reply via our new online reply facility. We look forward to serving you online.

The Top 100 Team

Sheringham Golf Club

www.kevinmurraygolfphotography.com
Princes Golf Course

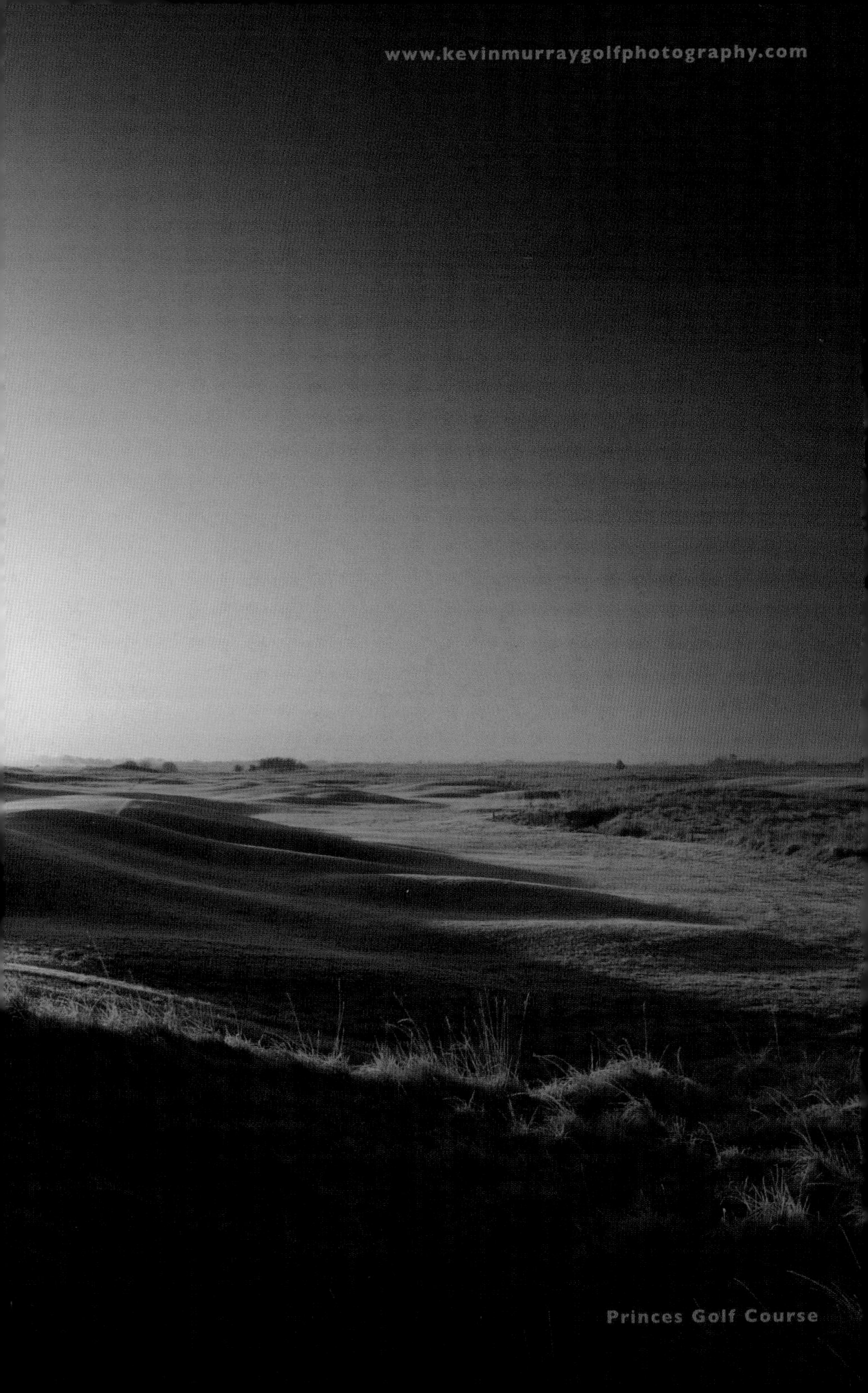

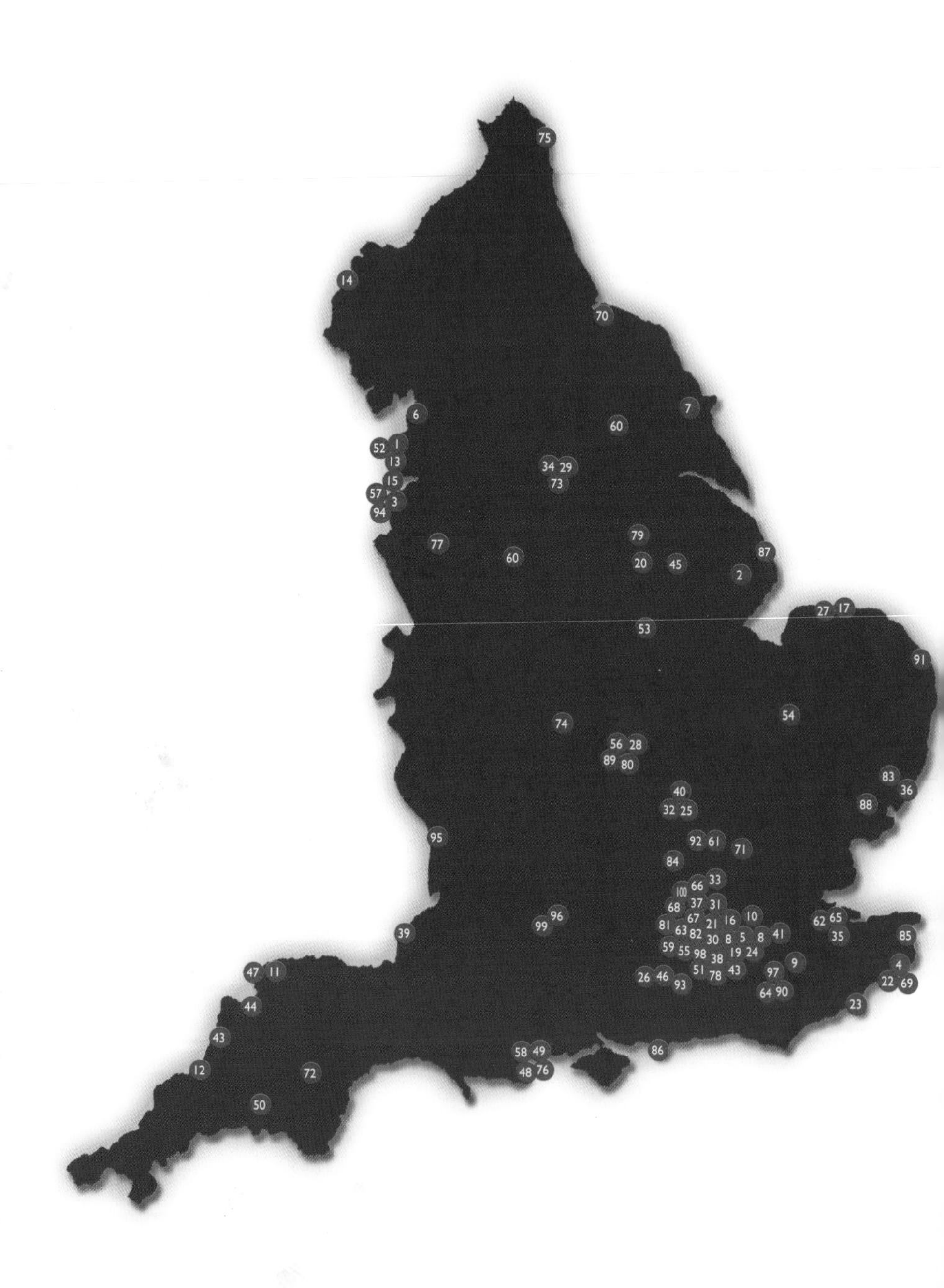
75
14
70
7
6
60
52
1
13
34
29
15
73
57
3
94
79
77
87
60
20
45
2
27
17
53
91
54
74
56
28
89
80
83
36
40
88
32
25
95
92
61
71
84
33
66
100
37
31
68
10
62
65
96
21
16
99
81
67
39
63
82
30
8
5
8
41
35
85
59
55
98
19
24
38
9
47
11
4
51
78
43
97
26
46
93
22
69
64
90
44
23
43
58
49
86
12
48
76
72
50

	Course
1	Royal Birkdale
2	Woodhall Spa (Hotchkin)
3	Royal Liverpool
4	Royal St George's
5	Sunningdale (Old)
6	Royal Lytham & St Annes
7	Ganton
8	Wentworth (West)
9	Walton Heath (Old)
10	St George's Hill
11	Saunton (East)
12	St Enodoc (Church)
13	Hillside
14	Silloth-on-Solway
15	Formby
16	Swinley Forest
17	Royal West Norfolk
18	Sunningdale (New)
19	Wentworth (East)
20	Notts
21	Berkshire (Red)
22	Royal Cinque Port
23	Rye (Old)
24	Worplesdon
25	Woburn (Duke's)
26	West Sussex
27	Hunstanton
28	Belfry (Brabazon)
29	Alwoodley
30	Hankley Common
31	Bearwood Lakes
32	Woburn (Marquess)
33	Grove
34	Moortown
35	Chart Hills
36	Aldeburgh
37	Berkshire (Blue)
38	West Hill
39	Burnham & Berrow
40	Woburn (Duchess)
41	Addington
42	Trevose (Championship)
43	Walton Heath (New)
44	Royal North Devon
45	Lindrick
46	Royal Ashdown Forest (Old)
47	Saunton (West)
48	Isle of Purbeck
49	Ferndown (Old)
50	St Mellion (Nicklaus)
51	Wisley (Garden & Mill)
52	Southport & Ainsdale

	Course
53	Luffenham Heath
54	Royal Worlington & Newmarket
55	Hindhead
56	Little Aston
57	West Lancs
58	Parkstone
59	Liphook
60	Fulford
61	Brocket Hall (Palmerston)
62	London Club (Heritage)
63	Woking
64	East Sussex National (West)
65	London Club (International)
66	Buckinghamshire
67	Wentworth (Edinburgh)
68	Stoke Park
69	Prince's
70	Seaton Carew
71	Hanbury Manor
72	Bovey Castle
73	Moor Allerton
74	Oxfordshire
75	Bamburgh Castle
76	Broadstone
77	Delamere Forest
78	Tandridge
79	Sherwood Forest
80	Forest of Arden (Arden)
81	North Hants
82	New Zealand
83	Woodbridge
84	Ashridge
85	Littlestone
86	Hayling
87	Seacroft
88	Ipswich (Main)
89	Copt Heath
90	East Sussex National (East)
91	Sheringham
92	Brocket Hall (Melbourne)
93	Crowborough Beacon
94	Wallasey
95	Ross-on-Wye
96	Manor House
97	Mannings Heath (Waterfall)
98	Burhill (Old)
99	Bowood G&CC
100	Moor Park (High)

Royal Birkdale

ROYAL BIRKDALE GOLF CLUB
Waterloo Road, Birkdale, Southport, Merseyside, PR8 2LX, England
Telephone: +44 (0) 1704 567920
Website: www.royalbirkdale.com
Architect: George Low, F.W. Hawtree and J.H. Taylor
Visitors: Contact in advance - Not Sat

Average Reviewers' Score:

Reviewers' Comments

Royal Birkdale is quite rightly England's best course – nothing really comes near to it for a complete all round test... Brilliant Open venue with acres of space in and around the sandhills on the course... Every hole is a unique and interesting championship test... Ver fair if you hit it straight... No weak holes, just a brilliant links course and a fair one too.. Wonderful layout which tests golfers of all abilities... Dunes serve to frame the holes as you play around, but not over the dunes. This gives each hole a unique, almost isolated feel... Surprised by blind tee shots at the 9th and 16th holes – they still allow this in the modern era of Open venues, marvellous! Diabolically placed bunkers seem to threaten you on every shot, making proper club selection a difficult task... If you enjoy golf, and especially if you enjoy links golf, you owe it to yourself to play this magnificent track... I dream of playing golf here for the rest of my life! How can a course be any better?

Kevin Murray

oyal Birkdale is a famous links and widely recognised for its fairness. If you hit ıe fairways, rarely will the ball be thrown off course as the fairways are laid out the flat-bottomed valleys between the towering dunes. These dunes, in turn, rovide superb viewing platforms for spectators.

irkdale has a superfluity of great golf holes. The 12th, a 183-yard par three is a assic hole and as natural as you can get. From a raised tee, the ball must carry cross a hollow, whilst avoiding four deep pot bunkers before coming to rest on narrow, raised green that is nestled the feet of tussocky sand dunes. The ar five 15th is Birkdale's longest hole ıd one of the most heavily bunkered n the course; knock it straight down ıe middle off the tee and then using long iron or a fairway wood, avoid ıe bunkers spread-eagled across the irway; chip it on and, bingo, an easy ve!

he experience can be torrid when the ind is up, with white horses kicking ıd rearing their heads in the Irish ea, crashing like kamikazes onto the each. But whatever the weather, Royal irkdale is a provocative place to play olf.

Brian G. Hodgkinson – Golf Professional writes:
'Tough but fair' may best describe Royal Birkdale.

Set amongst imposing sand dunes, it certainly has a completely natural feel that can be enjoyed by golfers of all abilities. From the daunting 1st hole to the unique setting of the famous 18th, which has set the scene for so many lasting and dramatic moments of past Ryder Cup matches and Open Championships, all players are challenged and encouraged to play their best golf ever.

For over 25 years, I have been greeting and meeting golfers from around the world. The overwhelming consensus is: 'if I could only play one course for the rest of my life, it would be Royal Birkdale'... a fitting tribute indeed.

'le

Woodhall Spa (Hotchkin)

WOODHALL SPA GOLF CLUB
The Broadway, Woodhall Spa, Lincs, LN10 6PU, England
Telephone: +44 (0) 1526 352511
Website: www.woodhallspagolf.com
Architect: Harry Vardon, Harry Colt & Colonel S.V. Hotchkin
Visitors: Contact in advance - handicap certificate required

Average Reviewers' Score:

Reviewers' Comments

Simply the yardstick by which I will measure any other inland course, and frankly none that I have played so far come close... An inland golf course that is quite simply the best in the UK and one that would rival Pine Valley... Determinedly rugged in its beauty, lined with gorse and ragged bunkers... Very good in places but by no means the best... It lacks interest (in terms of elevation change)... It's long, tight, sandy and varied... No real drama holes... A heathland course that every other should aspire to... To me it seems contrived and its claim to fame must be the bunkers... Layout is demanding with some superb bunkers that look as though they were created by World War II bombers... I thought bunker comments may be exaggerated but their depth and difficulty is actually understated... Will expose even the best-disguised weakness in your game... Represents exceptional value if you are a member of any club affiliated to the EGU... Truly excellent in every way... If you love golf, you'll love Woodhall.

Voodhall Spa is an oasis in the heart of Lincolnshire. Set amongst glorious pine, irch and broom, this heathland course is an absolute delight to play. The sandy ubsoil allows all-year-round golf, the springy turf making walking a real pleasure. eep your ball in play and do your best to avoid the heather, gorse and bunkers.

he Hotchkin is bunker heaven (or hell), notorious for its deep, cavernous sand raps. It is also helpful if you can hit the ball long and straight. Otherwise you will e presented with some very tough second shots.

t is definitely worth making the trip o play this gem and the green fee s tremendous value for money too especially if you are a member of an nglish golf club). And remember – the Hotchkin is undoubtedly one of the remier inland courses in the whole of he British Isles. Can you afford not to lay it?

Richard A Latham – Director of Operations writes:
The Hotchkin Course at Woodhall Spa is generally regarded as one of the finest heathland courses in the world. In fact, it has been consistently rated in the world's top fifty over the last seventy years.

Long carries over heather, deep cavernous bunkers and a wonderful variety of short and long holes are the main features of the course. Interestingly, there are only three par 3s, ranging from 148 yards to 209 yards, and the penalties for an errant tee shot can be severe. The greens are relatively flat, although there are some subtle borrows, and they're in good order throughout the year. Most of the course is built on sand so this is an excellent winter course.

Royal Liverpool

ROYAL LIVERPOOL GOLF CLUB
Meols Drive, Hoylake, Wirral, Merseyside, CH47 4AL, England
Telephone: +44 (0) 151 632 3101
Website: www.royal-liverpool-golf.com
Architect: George Morris, Harry Colt, Donald Steel
Visitors: Not Thu am or weekends – contact in advance

Average Reviewers' Score:

Reviewers' Comments

Had the ultimate privilege of playing Hoylake four days after the Open and couldn't have asked for more… It's a supreme test of golf… I have never before and probably never will putt on truer greens… Some would say it's flat and boring and I'd agree with flat but boring it certainly isn't…Are there many dunes? No. Does it matter? Definitely not… Really enjoyed the course and it was a decent test – inevitable wind and deep bunkers are really tricky… Bring your A game or you will be in trouble… Some genuinely stunning holes and the 10th and 11th stand out for me… Had a go at holing out from 190 yards on the 14th like Tiger did, guess what I missed! As good a test of your inner game as any I have come across… I can't wait to play here again… Clubhouse is beautiful with lots of history and a great lunch… Received a warm welcome at the course from all the staff… Thanks Hoylake for a wonderful Open Championship.

Kevin Murray

The Open Championship finally returned to Royal Liverpool in 2006 after a 39-year gap. Hoylake, as it is called by those in the know, has a long and illustrious history of playing host to the Open, and has now hosted eleven, its first in 1897. Founded in 1869, Hoylake is the second oldest seaside links course in England - only Royal North Devon is the more senior.

Donald Steel was commissioned to make alterations to the course ahead of the Open; these changes included a number of new greens, tees and bunkers. Work was completed in 2001 and Hoylake now stretches out in excess of 7,000 yards.

The land is unusually flat, offering little in the way of definition. Houses border three sides of the course and the Dee Estuary lies on the western side. When you get out onto the course, the undulations become more pronounced and, as you move away from the houses, the overall aesthetic improves. The holes alongside the shore (9th, 10th, 11th and 12th) are the most visually appealing and very challenging.

Without doubt, Royal Liverpool is a tough links. Only a couple of holes are in the dunes – otherwise there is little protection from the ever-changing wind. There is nothing artificial about the course. It represents a traditional, genuine test of golf and it was heart-warming to see that Hoylake examined the very best players in 2006. They came, they saw and Tiger conquered!

Donald Steel writes:
The last word belongs to Tom Simpson and the obituary which, by mutual agreement, Henry Longhurst wrote before Simpson's death. In discussing some of his philosophies about golf course architecture, Simpson declared that, to be any good, a golf course must have out-of-bounds. "I take it you regard Hoylake as the finest in England," enquired Longhurst.
"Without any doubt," came the unhesitating reply.

Royal St George's

ROYAL ST GEORGE'S GOLF CLUB
Sandwich, Kent, CT13 9PB, England
Telephone: +44 (0) 1304 613090
Website: www.royalstgeorges.com
Architect: William Laidlaw Purves, Frank Pennink
Visitors: Contact in advance - not at the weekend

Average Reviewers' Score:

Reviewers' Comments

A real must for any golfer... Price was a bit steep but I didn't care, I just wanted to hit a drive over the monster bunkers at the 4th... You can see traces of the relentless wind... As usual, the links wind will be the biggest challenge with some par 4s being 3-shotters and the two par 5s in range when it is behind... Lots of pot bunkers... Land in any of the fairway bunkers and it's a dropped shot... Firm greens and terrific fairways... Lots of up and down on the fairways and blind tee shots... Apart from having wonderful greens and a few innovative bunkers, this is not worth the money... Magic bunkering around the greens... Greens are absolutely huge, hard and fast... No real signature hole, except maybe the 4th... 10th is probably the hardest par four on the course... Old-fashioned golf and real fun too... You may be good enough to score better than the winner of the first Open held here... Great history, great tradition – must be played.

n 1887, the course opened for play and was named "St George's" after the English patron saint. After only seven years of play, in 1894, Sandwich hosted its first of 13 Open Championships. This was the first Open to be played outside Scotland.

The course is not a traditional out and back layout. In a similar style to Muirfield, each nine is broadly circular, a loose figure of eight. There is nothing artificial about Royal St George's; there is a natural look and feel to the course that blends beautifully into the surroundings, with wild flowers, dune grasses and the sweet song of the lark. Commanding views over Pegwell Bay and the white cliffs of Dover ensure an amazing experience.

Royal St George's has some unique features; thatched roof shelters, the red cross of St George on the flags, and that bunker on the 4th hole cut into a huge dune, the UK's tallest and deepest bunker.

Andrew Brooks – Head Professional writes:

My advice for those playing Royal St George's for the first time is to always aim at the middle of the greens and ignore pin placement. Being patient will pay dividends – this was certainly the case for Ben Curtis when he won the 2003 Open Championship. I gave him some advice about the nuances of our course, including, not to over borrow whilst putting. The rest is history.

My favourite holes include the 4th, where the bunker must be avoided at all costs with your tee shot. The par 3, 6th has a wonderful undulating green which is a fantastic putting surface and the tee shot at 14th is a real test with OOB all the way down the right hand side. The par 3 16th holds different memories – Tony Jacklin had the first televised hole-in-one here and Thomas Bjorn took three to escape the greenside bunker, waving goodbye to the 2003 Claret Jug in the process – if only he had have aimed for the middle of the green!

But my favourite shot must be the approach to the 8th hole with a mid iron when the pin is at the back of the green. I can assure you that you'll find a wonderful links experience waiting at Royal St George's.

Lee Brown

Sunningdale (Old) 5th

SUNNINGDALE GOLF CLUB
Ridgemount Road, Sunningdale, Berkshire, SL5 9RR, England
Telephone: +44 (0) 1344 621681
Website: www.sunningdale-golfclub.co.uk
Architect: Willie Park Junior, Harry Colt
Visitors: Contact in advance - Not Fri, Sat, Sun or public hols

Average Reviewers' Score:

Reviewers' Comments

One of the finest inland courses in GB&I… Play the Old before all others on your list of courses to play… 36 holes on the Old and the New at Sunningdale takes some beating… The Old is my favourite with a little more room off the tee and "big" greens… The turf is gorgeous and it's a course that is pleasing on the eye… This is real golf in a sublime setting where the staff take time for the visitor… Is the Old better than the New? It's like comparing rugby and football… This classic layout is very tight off the tee with heather and pine trees bordering every fairway… Enjoy that drive on the elevated 10th tee… Gets very busy in summer… It's pretty expensive to play here but it's cheaper than Wentworth and in my book Sunningdale is better… If I had to play one golf course only for the rest of my life – it would be a tough call – but I would say Sunningdale Old course

Stuart Abramson

The Old course at Sunningdale is one of the British Isles' most aesthetically ›leasing inland courses. Lined with pine, birch and oak trees, it is a magnificent ›lace to play golf. The emblem of the club is the oak tree, no doubt modelled on he huge specimen tree standing majestically beside the 18th green. It's incredible o believe that originally the golf course was laid out on barren, open land.

f you have already played the Old :ourse, you will surely remember the :levated 10th tee, a fabulous driving ıole and one of our all-time favourite ıoles. By the time you have putted ›ut on the 10th, you will be ready for 'efreshments at the excellent halfway ıut that sits welcomingly behind the ;reen. What sheer delight!

Many people regard Sunningdale as he perfect golfing venue. The Old ınd New courses taken together are ›robably the finest pair of golf courses ınywhere. On a sunny autumn day, walking on that perfect heathland turf, ;urely there is nowhere better to play ;olf with a few friends.

Keith Maxwell – Head Professional writes:
Sunningdale's Old and New courses sit side by side and provide two very different tests of golf.

The Old is much more tree-lined but still very much the heathland course it always has been. The layout is such that it allows the players to ease into the round with the opening holes being a fairly open par five followed by a tough par four, a short par four and uphill par three.

It is at this point that we appreciate the true beauty of Sunningdale as the 5th and 6th are set before us end to end. The 10th hole remains everyone's favourite; it's both eye catching and tough with the added bonus of our famous halfway hut. The closing holes very much epitomise Sunningdale with the backdrop of the double oak and Clubhouse.

Naithan Tucker

Royal Lytham & St Annes 6th

ROYAL LYTHAM & ST ANNES GOLF CLUB
Links Gate, St Annes on Sea, Lancashire, FY8 3LQ, England
Telephone: +44 (0) 1253 724206
Website: www.royallytham.org
Architect: Harry Colt, Herbert Fowler, Tom Simpson & C.K.Cotton
Visitors: Mon & Thu - Contact in advance

Average Reviewers' Score:

Reviewers' Comments

One word to describe the Lytham experience – *fantastic*! Had a wonderful experience, members were the most welcoming of all Open venues… Their 94-year-old Dormy house – it is a *must*… Honestly, this was *by far* the best golfing experience I have ever had… Fairly flat and uninteresting with very few memorable holes… Fantastic links course that asks all the right questions… A tough golf course – long, tight and relentless… Strategic bunkering, tricky and slick greens and a brutal closing stretch... 8th hole was my favourite; played to a raised green at the corner of the course… It gets relatively tight around the turn… Bunkers are deep and plentiful round the whole estate so don't expect to keep your sand wedge in the bag… Only letdown is the lack of sea views, otherwise it's as good as it gets… Staff were exceptionally welcoming… You owe i to yourself as a golfer to tread the same turf as Seve… Fantastic experience!

oyal Lytham & St Annes is the most northerly of the English championship links ourses, situated only 10 miles, as ie seagull flies, from its illustrious eighbour, Royal Birkdale.

he links is positioned – rather nusually – surrounded by red brick ouses and flanked on the west by ie railway line while the guardian 'ictorian clubhouse watches sternly ver the course. The conditioning f the course is exceptional and ot as rough and ready as many of s contemporaries. The ground is elatively even, except perhaps on couple of holes, where the land is ightly wrinkled.

'he course itself is extremely ough, only Carnoustie (on the ritish Open circuit) is thought o be tougher. The greens are rm, fast and true and the 1st is nique because this is the only par hree starting hole on the Open Championship circuit and it's a long ne, measuring 206 yards from the ack tees.

The Professional Team of Eddie Birchenough, Simon Avery, Ben Squires and Tim Rich writes:
At first sight, Royal Lytham & St Annes Golf Club doesn't strike one as a classic links, with neither sight nor sound of the sea. Despite being one of the shorter courses on the Open rota, Lytham retains its place as one of the most demanding due to its tight fairways, deep rough and 200 strategically placed bunkers.

Requiring accurate ball striking and a delicate short game, it is no surprise this course has crowned many great champions. From Seve Ballesteros prevailing over Nick Price on a glorious Monday in 1988 to Gary Player's left handed chip from the side of the clubhouse to claim victory in 1974. However, Royal Lytham probably remains most famous of all for Bobby Jones's miraculous second shot from the sandy wasteland on the left of the 17th to help snatch the Claret Jug from Al Watrous in 1926.

Set on a narrow strip of land amongst Lytham's red brick homes, the course may make no claim to being the prettiest of championship venues. However, as a supreme test of a golfer's all round skill, its position is assured at the very top of the list.

n McCann

Ganton

GANTON GOLF CLUB
Ganton, North Yorkshire, YO12 4PA, England
Telephone: +44 (0) 1994 710329 **Website:** www.gantongolfclub.com
Architect: Tom Chisholm, James Braid, Ted Ray, J.H. Taylor, Alister MacKenzie Tom Simpson and C.K. Cotton
Visitors: Via prior arrangement – not at weekends

Average Reviewers' Score:

Reviewers' Comments

Ganton is so understated, so subtle – apart from its bunkering... My favourite inland course... Probably the greatest inland course with links style in the world... A combination of links land in a heathland setting... Have never played a course and had to use my sand wedge so often – bunkers are so strategically placed (and often enormous) that you will do very well to go round here and avoid them... Need to be long and very straight. If you see your ball going toward the ever-present gorse, it is in the gorse... Every hole is a true challenge – even the short par 4 14th... Like all true classic courses, holes change direction all the way round and there are a couple of delightful surprises at the end thrown in for good measure... A real test, even for long hitters... The championship pedigree is exceptional... Any golfer who is serious about playing the great courses of the British Isles must play Ganton... Very friendly members... Rightly rated as highly as this... Well worth the trip.

Cédric Hannedouche

o classify Ganton as a heathland course is a misnomer – one could just as easily ategorise it as an inland links, as it's situated in the rural Vale of Pickering, nine iles from the sea. This sandy, gently undulating site was once a North Sea inlet. onsequently, it has all the characteristics of a links and a heathland course. ther way, it's a perfect place to play golf.

he bunkering is quite extraordinary, a real feature of the course. With over 100 unningly placed bunkers, some of which are simply huge, both in breadth and in epth, whilst others are small. Only lucky (or very good golfers) will avoid the nd traps at Ganton.

you blend the Old course at Walton eath with Woodhall Spa's Hotchkin ourse and then throw in a touch of luirfield, you've got Ganton. Occupying pen, windswept heathland, it's a upreme thinking man and woman's test f golf; the fast greens and firm fairways est the very best players. Various types f thick gorse, heather and broom ighlight the course during the spring nd summer months.

anton is a friendly club that opens its oors warmly to visitors (providing you ave a handicap). If you are a serious olfer and have never played here, we trongly recommend it.

James W. Finegan writes:
Playing Ganton is a starkly confrontational business. Hole after hole, shot after shot, without so much as a moment's let-up, it is golfer versus golf course. Never is there a free swing, where we can open the shoulders, "grip it and rip it." Always, catastrophe lurks, in either the sandy caverns or the great stands of gorse. At times we incline to believe that the entire course must have been dredged up out of a sea of gorse, an intractable expanse of potentially unplayable – and literally prickly – lies. As for the bunkers, 123 by actual count – many of them malevolently deep, their banks often gorse infested, some pits with revetted faces, a few with boarded faces, certain bunkers requiring steps in order to get in and out – these hazards fiercely stare us down at every turn.

n McCann

Wentworth (West)

8th

WENTWORTH CLUB
Virginia Water, Surrey, GU25 4LS, England
Telephone: +44 (0) 1344 842201
Website: www.wentworthclub.com
Architect: Harry Colt and Ernie Els
Visitors: Handicap certificate required – contact in advance

Average Reviewers' Score:

Reviewers' Comments

Wentworth is entertainment for any golfer playing well or badly... The whole place has a buzz... A lovely place to play golf and certainly has a bit of X-Factor... It's not the best in the country (it's not the best in the surrounding area), but you do get half way around and think, "Wow, this is Wentworth"... Expensive – but worth every penny... Expensive it is, but that's probably what sets it apart in the desirability stakes... Recent changes made by Ernie Els will need some time to settle in but the West has certainly been toughened up and tightened up... Water at the 8th is now a real problem cutting all the way around the green... A fantastic design and, without doubt, it is a classic but there are better heathland courses in the area... Recommend playing in winter, it's cheaper... I really enjoyed it and will be returning again shortly... Great course, great atmosphere, great experience... Wentworth scores very highly on ambience... Loved every minute... One of my all-time favourites.

Kevin Murray

ıe West course at Wentworth is the most famous of the Surrey heath and
ːather courses and is also the most
levised course in Britain. Designed
1926 by Harry Colt, it's a relative
›ungster in the scheme of things as
any of Surrey's famous sand-belt
›urses were established around the
ırn of the 19th century.

/hen you step onto the first tee, you
ill feel an overwhelming sense of
miliarity. It is definitely a place most
ːople would be more than happy
› call home and play the monthly
edal here for the rest of their lives.
he holes weave their way through
›rinklings of heather and across
ːntly undulating terrain. Mature oaks,
nes and silver birch trees line each
ıd every fairway.

his is a truly classy golf course and
's a tough one too, especially after
·nie Els gave the West a new set of
ːeth in 2006. It now measures more
ıan 7,300 yards from the tips. With
) new bunkers and some stunning
ːw tees, the Burma Road is now a
ːrious 21st century challenge.

Ernie Els writes:
Everyone knows how much I love the West Course at Wentworth. I just have so many great memories from the tournaments I've played here over the years. This is also the place that we choose to call home. It's a wonderful part of the world to live, with everything we could ever want on our doorstep.

It's a great privilege for me, then, to be given the opportunity to refine and modernise the West Course. The brief was not to change the character of the golf course. That would be a crime! But to ensure it remains a fitting challenge for the professional who plays in the tournaments, as well as the amateur golfer.

The fact is the West Course did not play as Harry Colt intended and the changes address that. I needed to ensure that amateurs can still enjoy the course for what it is – a great piece of golf course design. After all, for 50 weeks of the year, it is amateurs who play this golf course. But for the other two weeks of the year, when the prestigious tournaments come to town, I think it's important this great old golf course remains a test for the best.

Walton Heath (Old)

9th

WALTON HEATH GOLF CLUB
Deans Lane, Walton on the Hill, Surrey, KT20 7TP, England
Telephone: +44 (0) 1737 812380
Website: www.whgc.co.uk
Architect: Herbert Fowler
Visitors: Contact in advance - weekends limited

Average Reviewers' Score:

Reviewers' Comments

I love Walton Heath – either course – but the Old is special, very special… Outside of the British Open courses I've not been to a club steeped in as much history… Lovely course that is pure and simple heathland… Has all the attributes that you would expect from great courses – natural layout out, strategic bunkering, penal rough, heather, and a varied selection of holes and of course firm and true greens… Opens up to a poor start with an average 1st hole, cross the road and it soon opens up… Challenging long par 4s, well guarded par 3s and par 5s you cannot attack without perfect placement off the tee… Some of the holes felt quite cramped… Sensational greens, great fairways, tough bunkers – ooh and don't forget the heather, but do your best to avoid it! I enjoyed the whole experience and it was followed up by a stellar lunch… Has one of the most charming putting greens you will ever see… Play Walton Heath for all that is good about English heathland golf.

Andy Taylor

Valton Heath is where links golf meets inland golf. There is no salty whiff of ea air, but the course plays and feels like a seaside links. A profusion of heather tripes the edge of the fairways. In the summer, when the heather is in flower, it is n absolute delight to look at, but a real challenge to play out of. The greens are ue and fast and the undulations make it tough to read the lines and the pace of utts.

his is a course that favours the lower handicap golfer. Some of the carries across ne heather are quite lengthy and if you don't hit the fairways, you can often wave oodbye to your ball. There are some eally strong holes on the Old course one of the best of the outward nine the 5th, a cracking 391-yard par four nat demands a solid drive that must void the thick, tangly heather shrouding ne fairway. A mid-iron approach shot vill find the green, amply guarded y bunkers left and right. The last nree holes are especially challenging, specially the 16th, a 510-yard par five.

Valton Heath has hosted many nportant competitions, not least the 981 Ryder Cup. Unfortunately, Europe vas thrashed 9½ - 18½ by America, nanks to the likes of Watson and Jicklaus. For serious golfers, this is a ntastic venue for a golf day.

Ken Macpherson – Professional writes:

"A links course laid out inland" was how the Old Course was described in 1904 and its layout is very similar to The Old Course at St Andrews in that is eight holes out, a loop of three, and seven holes back.

The firm, closely-cut turf is ideal for the run-up approach shot and the design of the course, together with the ever-present wind, encourages this style of old fashioned golf.

Although the course is a long one, the fast fairways produce additional run provided that they can be found off the tee. Few courses anywhere can lay claim to the description "A driver's course" more than Walton Heath.

uart Abramson

St George's Hill

ST GEORGE'S HILL GOLF CLUB

Average Reviewers' Score:

Golf Club Road, St George's Hill, Weybridge, Surrey, KT13 0NL, England
Telephone: +44 (0) 1932 847758
Website: www.stgeorgeshillgolfclub.co.uk
Architect: Harry Colt
Visitors: Contact in advance – handicap cert required

Reviewers' Comments

The stunning clubhouse has the feel of a really comfy pair of old slippers... Course oozes charm and character and is beautifully natural... Wonderfully laid out, following the natural contours superbly... Three excellent loops of nine through undulating pine forests and heather... A great mix of fantastic driving holes, well-placed hazards and wonderfully sculpted greens – this really is a feast... All of the holes were a great test, well bunkered and with excellent greens that had many subtle and not so subtle borrows... Every hole is a challenge, with a mixture of long par 3s, some short par 4s and testing par 5s... Not a very testing golf course for the better player... Forget all that nonsense about it being a short course, all the Colt classics are... Turf is lovely and promotes a nice strike... More affordable than Sunningdale and Wentworth... Treated with warmth and friendliness by the staff and members... An all-round wonderful golfing experience... Looking forward to my next round here.

t George's Hill is the prettiest of the many heathland courses on the Surrey/ erkshire sand belt and, in our opinion, one of the very best. In 1911, a local uilder came up with an original idea to build luxury fairway-side houses and by hance, Harry Colt was the chosen architect. The course opened for play in 1913 nd it is considered to be Colt's greatest work.

he most notable difference between St George's Hill and the heathland layouts this area is the terrain. The land here sweeps and undulates like a rollercoaster nd Harry Colt used these dramatic elevation changes superbly in his design.

he spectacular panorama from the front of the clubhouse, or the pavilion as was originally called, totally whets your appetite. It is one of those views that rabs you and makes your heart pound in excited anticipation. You cannot help ut want to get out onto the first tee as quickly as possible.

mongst the grandiose setting is inherent charm and beauty. The houses beside he fairways have style and never impose and, if anything, they are complementary nd add to the amazing St George's Hill experience.

Head Professional – Tony Rattue writes:
St George's Hill is a wonderfully testing layout with fir trees, sand and heather. These are beautiful things in themselves and the ingredients from which inland courses should be made. The prettiest courses are also the best and certainly one of the prettiest and the best is St George's Hill.

Saunton (East)

SAUNTON GOLF CLUB
Braunton, North Devon, EX33 1LG, England
Telephone: +44 (0) 1271 812436
Website: www.sauntongolf.co.uk
Architect: Herbert Fowler
Visitors: Book in advance – handicap certificate required

Average Reviewers' Score:

Reviewers' Comments

Far and away the best course we played while staying the west of England... Standing at the first tee is quite an experience... Classic links extend all around you as you reach for the driver... Simply magnificent golf... A course with so much potential – the 18 holes are near perfect... Hard fast fairways and greens, wispy long rough and great routing... Length is not the problem but trouble lurks just off every fairway... Found the course not overlong from the white markers – only the 1st, 4th and 14th (toughest hole) made us struggle but there is relief in the aptly named 5th 'Tiddler'... Layout/set-up is good and you do seem to be 'on your own hole' a lot of the time... Selection of par 3s, 4s and a couple of 5s are great... Really enjoyed ourselves and our only regret was not having the time or stamina for the West course... If Saunton was located in East Lothian, it would perhaps be considered to be one of the greatest courses on the planet.

Saunton Golf Club

aunton is located on the beautiful unspoilt North Devon coast. On the edge of ideford Bay and the estuary of the River Taw, lie the Braunton Burrows. Unesco as designated the sand dunes at Braunton Burrows of international importance nd it is the first site in the UK to become a biosphere reserve.

he East course, laid out in 1897, runs hrough a small part of this amazing xpanse of sand dunes. Herbert Fowler dded a bit of redesign magic in 1919 nd very little has changed since. Fowler ook full advantage of the natural errain, routing the holes through the unes with skill. Saunton is his finest easide creation and Harry Vardon oved it, saying: "I would like to retire to aunton and do nothing but play golf for leasure."

's a tough golf course. The East has ight par fours over 400 yards long and nly two par fives. Scoring well is very ifficult, even more so now that the 2nd ole – once a short par five – has been engthened to almost 530 yards. There re two excellent short par threes, which demand accuracy, and there's the ough 207-yard 17th hole, which often eeds a decent crack with a wood.

Albert MacKenzie – Club Professional writes:
Saunton East is a truly wonderful links venue, set in traditional links terrain, and is widely acclaimed as the finest seaside course never to have hosted The Open. The golf course bares its teeth early on with the opening 4 holes totalling over one mile in length! By the time you reach the 5th tee it often seems like you've completed a marathon, never mind a mile.

The Par 3s, 5 and 13, are both less than 150 yards in length, but will test the best with their undulating features. Henry Longhurst had the 16th hole in his "Best 18" on the British Isles and it easy to see why. The East course will reward a good driver of the ball and the design of the course will allow for frequent use of this club should you so wish. This is simply links golf at its finest and should not be missed.

aul Edwards

St Enodoc (Church)

ST ENODOC GOLF CLUB
Rock, Wadebridge, Cornwall, PL27 6LD, England
Telephone: +44 (0) 1208 862200
Website: www.st-enodoc.co.uk
Architect: James Braid
Visitors: Contact in advance – handicap certificate required

Average Reviewers' Score

Reviewers' Comments

Wherever you live, it's worth the trip to Cornwall just to play St Enodoc... I can recall every hole – a sign of a truly memorable golf course... Amazing views from virtually every hole as well as an excellent test of golf (particularly in the wind)... Good value for money and full of excitement with fairways that look like rippled waves... The rollercoaster of 'sporty' holes relieved me of my thoughts of having mastered this game. I blame the scenery for distracting me at almost every tee box, fairway and green... Played badly and loved every minute of it! Take a moment to visit the church, if possible. Visit the grave of Betjeman, recite the famous poem and pray for a birdie or two, to restore your golfing soul... One of the best finishes in links golf... It's a dream come true for anyone who enjoys golf and holds a current handicap certificate... Experience is magical, almost trance-like... Truly a privilege to have played this jewel... St Enodoc is one of my personal favourite courses.

t Enodoc Golf Club is located at the royal sailing town of Rock, the links verlooking the Camel Estuary and the picturesque harbour of Padstow beyond. 'he Church course at St Enodoc takes its name from the tiny 13th century lace of worship that stands to the right of the 10th green. In the middle of the 9th century, a fierce storm completely covered the church in sand and it was ventually extricated in 1863.

:'s a quixotic links, set amidst towering sand dunes clad with tufts of wild ea grasses. The fairways undulate and ripple just as if the sea had ebbed only noments ago. We have to own up – this is one of our favourite links courses ecause the terrain is entirely natural. The dunes are so pronounced that you annot help but feel humbled, the holes are varied and charming and, finally, so nuch of the experience is memorable.

'here are many great holes, but the 6th is a bit of a collector's item, a hole of bsolute uniqueness, a blind drive followed by a blind mid iron second shot vhich must carry over a confrontational sand dune called "Himalayas". This tands some 100 yards out, guarding the hidden green. Let's be honest, this is an normous dune, worthy of its name, rising up over 75 feet high. Make sure you et your club selection right and that you strike the ball cleanly!

your ball happens to come to rest in ne churchyard after a wayward shot, eep an eye out for John Betjeman's eadstone. The Poet Laureate lies uried amidst his favourite seaside ourse. After a rare birdie on the 13th, e penned his famous poem "Seaside iolf."

James W. Finegan writes:
I suspect that if a genie were to appear before me at this moment with an offer to transport me magically to any course in the world, I just might choose this nonpareil on the wild north coast of Cornwall.

od Wiltshire

Hillside

HILLSIDE GOLF CLUB
Hastings Road, Hillside, Southport, Merseyside, PR8 2LU, England
Telephone: +44 (0) 1704 567169
Website: www.hillside-golfclub.co.uk
Architect: Fred Hawtree, Donald Steel
Visitors: Contact in advance – not weekends

Average Reviewers' Score:

Reviewers' Comments

What a course! Why is this course not rated higher as it deserves to be right up there amongst the very top rated tracks? I can only agree with all the reviews before that Hillside is a great course and for less than half the money of Royal Birkdale it is great value... Absolutely FANTASTIC golf course... If you are in Southport and only get the opportunity to play one course then play Hillside... Loved every moment of my four hours on the course...The back 9 is possibly the very best in England... And then the back nine – what a treat! Elevated tees abound with immaculate sleepered stepping and closely mown grass banks – very classy... Putting surfaces have grass replaced with green velvet – only kidding, but it seemed that way, they were so good! The 10th is described as possibly the best par three in GB&I – easy to see why... Lovely welcoming members – cannot wait to go back and experience this course again... Great experience indeed... This is a future Open Course in waiting... Golf heaven without doubt.

Kevin Murray

here are eight top-notch seaside courses between St Annes and Liverpool and
any people believe that this is the best stretch of linksland in the British Isles. It
certainly England's links golfing Mecca.

illside is an underrated gem, separated only by a footpath, but hiding in the
adow of its noble next-door neighbour, Royal Birkdale. The railway line
parates Hillside from Southport and Ainsdale, another superb but relatively
known links.

oday's layout is very different to the original Hillside that was founded in 1911.
he club acquired some new land in the
960s and Fred Hawtree extensively
modelled the course, making major
anges to the back nine. The front
ne has always been highly regarded
d plays over relatively flat ground,
ut it's the homeward nine that is really
ecial and is frequently bracketed
ongside Ballybunion because the holes
pple and undulate through the giant
unes.

illside has many strong and individual
oles but the 11th has everything going
r it. A reachable par five of just over
00 yards that doglegs left, the elevated
e provides a panoramic view of the
ole in play and many other holes too,
ot only at Hillside but also at Royal
irkdale and Southport & Ainsdale.

Brian Seddon – PGA Professional – Hillside Golf Club

Although Hillside is Royal Birkdale's near neighbour, it is never in its shadow and many would rank both courses equally. Hillside is set amongst glorious sandhills and also several holes are tree-lined.

The back nine were routed through huge sand dunes and these holes combine to provide a thrilling and dramatic closing sequence which is regarded by many as one of golf's best inward stretches.

Hillside is not only a regular Open Qualifying course but the club also played host to the PGA Championship in 1982, which was Tony Jacklin's last notable tour victory.

Silloth on Solway

SILLOTH ON SOLWAY GOLF CLUB
The Club House, Silloth on Solway, Cumbria, CA7 4BL, England
Telephone: +44 (0) 16973 31304
Website: www.sillothgolfclub.co.uk
Architect: Davy Grant, Willie Park Jnr
Visitors: Contact in advance

Average Reviewers' Score

Reviewers' Comments

It's the best course I have ever played... Lovely scenic views over the Solway... A wonderful links course... Starts out with a drive over a sand dune with the green set below... A good, old fashioned out and back layout with a real wild, untamed feel to the terrain – it's very natural and nothing is tricked up here... Holes have a great variety of twists and turns, and every hole turns out to be much more of a test than you would think by looking at the card... Blind carries and the vagaries of the links bounce test the players resolve... Short par three 9th is one of the great short par threes in the world... You will not get better value anywhere in the UK for a Top 50 course... If I had to play my last ever round of golf you'd find me on the 1st tee at Silloth on Solway... It really is remote jewel that shines brightly in the northwest corner of England... Golf as it should be.

Jim McCann

lloth on Solway Golf Club was founded in 1892, with the help of Railway ompany money. Davy Grant and Willie Park Jnr. originally designed it and is a club famous for its affiliation with ladies' golf. Silloth has parliamentary onnections too. Viscount Willie Whitelaw was the Club President until his death 1999.

ou have to make an extra special effort to get to Silloth because it is located one of the most remote and isolated aces in England, at the mouth of the olway Firth. But the winding road trip is uly worthwhile.

Vith heather and gorse adding brilliant lashes of seasonal colour, Silloth is cracking links golf course. When the ind blows, it's unlikely that you will play your handicap. Even on a calm day, ou'll find it tough. "It is also the home f the winds," wrote Darwin, "when I as there the wind did not blow really ard, but hard enough to make a fool of e." Finding the tight greens is no mean at either, and when you do, they are ough to read with their subtle borrows.

's well worth the time (and the money) get to Silloth and once you get there, ou won't want to leave. You are at one f the best value golf courses in the hole of the British Isles.

Jonathan Graham – Head Professional writes:
Silloth is an enchanting course and the very epitome of the phrase "hidden gem".

Each hole has its own charm and unique feel and will test all your skills especially your short game. While obviously an advantage, length is not terribly important at Silloth; there is a premium on accuracy. Miss the fairways and you will be punished and if you manage to find the fairway chances are you won't have a very flat lie to cope with.

The signature hole is the 13th, which at 518 yards is not a long par five by modern standards. But it is a wonderfully testing hole, a real risk or reward decision. And when you eventually reach the green, you are greeted by stunning views across the Solway Firth and Lake District.

edric Hannedouche

FORMBY GOLF CLUB *Average Reviewers' Score*

Golf Road, Formby, Merseyside, L37 1LQ, England
Telephone: +44 (0) 1704 872164
Website: www.formbygolfclub.co.uk
Architect: Willie Park, James Braid, Hawtree and Taylor, Donald Steel
Visitors: Contact in advance

Reviewers' Comments

The strength of Formby is the layout. Every hole is different... Fantastic course and you wouldn't expect to find trees on that stretch of the coast… The fir tree emblem on ball markers, hole flags and such-like tells you all you need to know about Formby – it is dominated by trees of the pine variety which are used to good effect throughout the course… A superb course and what a deal in early November… Good condition with the greens true and quick… The best greens we played on too... Greens were such that your putting improved because their quality and pace demanded full concentration… Marvellous conditioning and heavenly hole routing in an anti-clockwise circle… Was a great challenge with well-placed bunkers… Much of a heathland feel to it...A real beast from the back tees… Holes 7 to 9 were particularly strong, with hole 7 the pick of the trio… Formby was a very fine place to play and a double bill of golf here and at Hillside would be a great day out.

Kevin Murray

ɔrmby is a unique course as the holes are routed in a huge anti-clockwise circle ·ound the Formby Ladies' Club which sits slap bang in the middle of the men's ɔurse. The first three holes follow the railway line, the 4th turns and heads out ɔwards the Irish Sea and at the turn, we meander back home, zigzagging up and ɔwn along the way.

he club has hosted a number of important amateur events over the years and ayed host to the 2004 Curtis Cup. After an exciting finish, the United States ıccessfully retained the trophy, winning 0-8. The Amateur Championship was ayed here on three occasions; José aria Olazábal emerged as the 1984 ·inner.

ay Formby when you have been ıfficiently beaten up by the other ·indy links courses around Liverpool ıd Southport, but don't be fooled ıto thinking that this course is easy. It ertainly is not. Bunkering is strategic, ıe undulating fairways are very much ıks-like, the rough is strewn with eather and the pines provide an ement of park-like protection from ıe wind. Formby will suit both links ›vers and the player who prefers the ɔftness of inland golf; both these camps ·ill arrive contentedly at the 19th ·atering hole.

Gary H. Butler – Head Professional writes:
Formby is a magnificent golf links, set quite uniquely amidst a profusion of pine trees, and it's the centrepiece in the string of world-class golf courses that stretch between Southport and Liverpool.

There are so many great golf holes that it is difficult to single any out, but the par five 8th is one of my favourites, requiring careful thought and a strategy. If you can hit it long and straight, this hole may yield a birdie. If you are offline, you'll be in the trees and struggling for par. The 12th is a beautiful hole visually but the little par three 16th can be a card-wrecker. With three deep pot bunkers and a green that slopes away from you, a par here is always a good score.

ɛvin Murray

Swinley Forest

SWINLEY FOREST GOLF CLUB
Coronation Road, Ascot, Berkshire, SL5 9LE, England
Telephone: +44 (0) 1344 874979
Website: None
Architect: Harry Colt
Visitors: By invitation only

Average Reviewers' Score

Reviewers' Comments

This is one of those revered, must-play courses that I was dying to play simply because of its reputation and exclusivity... Having played many of the best heathland courses, I can say that this is one of them... We played a two ball in just over three hours. It was bliss... Despite the seemingly short nature of the course – apart from the two par 5s and two of the par 4s – the rest of the par 4s were all very solid, and the par 3s were mostly long and tricky... Par 3s are the highlight, all requiring a good iron shot... 5th was my favourite hole – a gently half-moon dogleg from a lovely raised tee with the only small lake on the course two thirds of the way down on the right... Very springy sandy soil and terrain which is more undulating than you would expect... A treat that should not be missed if you are given the opportunity... Old-school clubhouse adds the to the enjoyment... If you can get an invitation, you have to play it.

winley Forest is an absolutely charming golf course on the famous Surrey/ erkshire sand belt, but it's a club that is frozen in time, exclusive, unusual nd totally eccentric. In fact, you would be hard pressed to describe it as a onventional golf club: there is no captain and despite being in existence for early 100 years, no history, except in its members' heads. Only recently have corecards been printed, holes allocated par figures, and competitions introduced or Swinley's distinguished gentlemen members.

arry Colt designed the layout and the course opened for play in 1909, reputedly olt's favourite and finest design. One of the many delights of Swinley is the nbience and the fact that it's unpretentious. It has none of the glamour of its ear neighbours Sunningdale and Wentworth, but what Swinley Forest does have bags of style.

Ve will make no bones about it – Swinley is a beautiful course. The short, one-hot holes are simply outstanding. The site/position of the greens sets Swinley part from many other courses. Although the yardage is only a little over 6,000 ards, the par of 68 makes it a real challenge.

you are lucky enough to play in late spring, look out for the rhododendrons ctually you can't miss them), they are mply breathtaking. Combine this with wathes of purple heather and lovely pringy fairways winding their way hrough mature pines and this really is a pecial place. Drop a letter in the post the secretary by way of introduction, r maybe telephone him. Who knows, e might let you play this amazing rivate members' course.

James W. Finegan writes:
Swinley is very short – 6,062 yards. Par is 69 in this interesting mix of eleven two-shotters, five par threes, and two par fives. Fairways are broad, forced carries are not cruel and bunkering inclines to be light. Heather, however, seems to be everywhere that grass is not.

ndy Taylor

Royal West Norfolk

ROYAL WEST NORFOLK GOLF CLUB
Brancaster, Norfolk, PE31 8AX, England
Telephone: +44 (0) 1485 210223
Website: None
Architect: Holcombe Ingleby
Visitors: Contact in advance – restricted at weekends

Average Reviewers' Score

Reviewers' Comments

Without a doubt, the best golf course in the British Isles... Wonderful experience - Felt as if I had gone back in time... A course of abundant character and majesty but despair, that it remains in constant danger of tidal destruction... Even a bad round is made enjoyable by the wonderful views... Beautiful, unpredictable, tough and friendly, and the added charm of numerous well behaved Black Labradors and Springer Spaniels accompanying many of the golfers... One will have to search hard to find a hole more intelligently designed than the 3rd or more picturesque than the 8th and 9th... Brancaster is a challenge to both your physical and mental game – it's a golfing game of chess, and you are constantly under fear of "checkmate" from the deep, sleeper-faced bunkers, hard and long rough, wind and water, delightful! The epitome of golfing tradition... Time-warp golf... Unique within the British Isles... The soul of this course is hard to define but easy to feel... Magnificent.

oyal West Norfolk Golf Club is a classic and nothing much has changed here
or 100 years. Squeezed beautifully between Brancaster Bay and the salt marshes,
truly is a peaceful golf links, except when the wind blows and boy, is the wind
racing here!

heck the tide times before you plan
our trip. The course plays on a narrow
trip of links-land which gets cut off at
igh tide, turning it into an island. If you
re lucky enough to play the course
uring high tide, you are in for a real
eat; the downside is that you will need
lenty of golf balls.

Out on the course, you feel delightfully
olated; often all you can hear are the
eductive sound of the wind, the seagulls,
he clinking of stays and the flapping
f boat sails. Essentially, the course is
traditional out and back links; huge
eeper-faced bunkers, fast greens and
hat beautiful links turf. A magical place
o play golf.

Simon Rayner – PGA Professional writes:
Royal West Norfolk Golf Club is discreetely situated on the North Norfolk coast, at the end of a tidal road. The course is surrounded by land preserved by The National Trust, including a beautiful sandy beach. The driving range is positioned on a Site of Special Scientific Interest (SSSI) as it's home to thousands of migrating birds and the wildlife that frequents the salt marshes.

The course moves away from the clubhouse and is played entirely on a sand spit, which stretches from Brancaster to Brancaster Staithe Harbour. It's pretty much nine holes out and nine holes back with traditional tight lies on the fairways, medium-sized greens and some cavernous sleepered bunkers. The addition of tidal flooding onto parts of the course make it a true test of golf whilst adding to the delight of this golfing experience.

mon Rayner

Sunningdale (New)

SUNNINGDALE GOLF CLUB
Ridgemount Road, Sunningdale, Berkshire, SL5 9RR, England
Telephone: +44 (0) 1344 621681
Website: www.sunningdale-golfclub.co.uk
Architect: Harry Colt
Visitors: Contact in advance - Not Fri, Sat, Sun or public hols

Average Reviewers' Score

Reviewers' Comments

The New is perhaps the most underrated layout in the country and it does not get the accolades it deserves... Played here on many occasions and a word about the club itself, stunning... Sunningdale really has style and it doesn't really matter whether you play the Old or the New, they are both first class courses... It's not that new really, dating back to the 1920s, but its routing is exemplary and bunker placement both cunning and cruel... It's challenging and plays on higher ground... A driver's course and if you get it away well off the tee, the chances are you'll score well...A tremendous test of golf... Numerous doglegs make the New a challenge and it helps if you can shape the ball in both directions... A strategic course... Either way, both Old and New are both superb, but for me, the New just has the edge... Sunningdale is a club anyone would be proud tc be a member of... Best 36-hole experience, bar none.

aken together, the New and Old courses at Sunningdale represent the finest 6 holes of golf in the whole of the British Isles. The same architect who made nodifications to Sunningdale's Old course, Harry Colt, designed the New course, vhich opened for play in 1923 to meet the ever-increasing demand for golf.

'his is a superb driving course for it is more open than the Old; the trees do not ncroach quite so much. Having said this, the New demands long carries from ts elevated tees over heathery terrain to narrow fairways. The club has been ollowing a programme of regeneration hat has involved the felling of a number of trees, thereby allowing the heather o return. In addition, this has cleared he way for long lost views to reappear cross to Chobham Common in the outh.

Many people will come to Sunningdale hell-bent on playing the Old course, but f it's a real athletic challenge you are fter, you will get severely tested on he rugged 6,700-yard par 70 New, a ougher, more rounded test of golf than he Old. So far, nobody has yet managed o better Jack Nicklaus's course record of 67, which is a testament to the echnical test that the New course hrows up.

Keith Maxwell – Head Professional writes:

Sunningdale's Old and New courses sit side by side and provide two very different tests of golf.

The New is perhaps a more challenging test and, unlike the Old, starts as it means to go on with a long uphill par four which is followed by a par three, short par four and the 4th – a long testing par four. From this point onwards the course does not let up until perhaps the 18th – par five – finish.

The New has always been much more exposed to the elements and defends itself with five great par threes. This is a great example of Harry Colt's architecture. As a result of these two great courses, Sunningdale has always been a place that demands and rewards good golf.

Stuart Abramson

Wentworth (East)

WENTWORTH CLUB
Virginia Water, Surrey, GU25 4LS, England
Telephone: +44 (0) 1344 842201
Website: www.wentworthclub.com
Architect: Harry Colt
Visitors: Handicap certificate required – contact in advance

Average Reviewers' Score:

Reviewers' Comments

The beauty of the East course is that it gives you all the style and quality of the West but you have a fairer chance of playing to your handicap... It seems more natural and prettier than the West... What a treat it was – like most things at Wentworth, it has got style and class... Shorter than its illustrious counterpart but still as tight, just as pretty and a lot less busy... Fairly short in places... Par 3s are all varied and testing... 11th is one of the great par 4s, left to right off the tee, across classic Colt bunkers followed by a right to left draw into a tiered green... Hard to believe when you play it that there are two other courses so close by... Add the East to your list of courses to play... Don't rush to Wentworth and make straight for the West, this is equally worth the money... If you get an invitation grab it, and it's a darn sight cheaper in the winter.

he West is the course that everybody rushes to play, but the East is more sandy, ıtimate and charming.

ı terms of length, it's relatively short, measuring 6,200 yards from the back tees, ut it's an exceedingly pleasant walk on the springy turf and the lowly par of 68 ill make playing to handicap a serious challenge. There's only one par five, but ıere are five par fours measuring in excess of 400 yards. It's the East's collection f five short holes that stand out: they are simply outstanding par threes.

'he East course occupies the central area of the Wentworth estate with the ewer Edinburgh course now sitting on ıe eastern side. It is a very special and ıtimate experience, as many people will lready know. The enclosed woodland etting confuses your sense of direction where only one hole is generally in iew and they seem to zigzag all over he place. It always comes as a pleasant urprise when we reach the halfway house vhere we can have a drink and draw a leep breath before we take on the 7th, an ppealing, but challenging, long par three.

The late Michael Williams former Telegraph Golf Correspondent:
Though perhaps overshadowed by the major events that are held on the West, Wentworth's East course is, in fact, the senior of the two.

The existing first hole on the West, which is sometimes referred to as the Burma Road, was the original opening hole on the East, the second then being played to the East's present first green. Otherwise the two courses have always gone their separate ways. While Wentworth's East is much shorter with a standard scratch score of 70 as opposed the West's 74, it is a first class course in its own right and, to perhaps the less able golfers, probably more enjoyable.

NOTTS GOLF CLUB
Average Reviewers' Score:

Hollinwell, Kirby-in-Ashfield, Nottinghamshire, NG17 7QR, England
Telephone: +44 (0) 1623 753225
Website: www.nottsgolfclub.co.uk
Architect: Willie Park Jnr, John H. Taylor
Visitors: Contact in advance – weekdays only – handicap cert required

Reviewers' Comments

One of the unsung gems of inland golf… Fantastic variation with holes cut through valley and elevated tee shots galore… It now measures a whopping 7,213 yards from the blue tees… This course is unbelievably difficult… 2nd and 3rd holes are the pick of the front nine with the 3rd green by the clubhouse… Smooth fast and true greens, narrow fairway and wicked wispy rough make Notts a course suited to the low handicapper… Each hol has its own features and charms, and as you walk round the golf course, you never want the round to end… Do take a look at the wonderful par 13th from that top back tee… Greens were as good as any I have played but beware of the speed and undulations… A dream for very good putters… Very fair test of golf… Clubhouse is one of the best I've been in, very old and spacious with plenty of interesting photos and trophies… Highly recommended and reasonably priced.

lotts Golf Club is also known as Hollinwell because there is a holy well located nongst the trees close to the 8th fairway. Water from the well is said to lend uch needed strength to the golfer, especially during the heat of summer. One f the British Isles' finest inland golf courses, Notts opened for play in 1887, riginally designed by Willie Park Jnr. Modifications (primarily to bunkering) were ter made by John H Taylor, to whom the club paid the princely sum of five uineas for his services!

he course plays across wonderfully undulating ground where some of the irways sweep through wooded hillsides and where others run through heather, rn and gorse clad valleys. Unusually, iere are a number of varieties of orse at Notts, and even in the depths f winter, you will find some in flower.

lotts feels very much like heathland he soil is sandy and the turf is pongy), but it also has a moorland avour and a touch of woodland. espite the varied landscape, this tractive course comes together really ell and actually gets better and better s you progress from hole to hole. It is so worth mentioning that a great deal f effort is being put in to encourage ie heather to return to its former ory.

The following passage was published in Henry Cotton's Guide to Golf In The British Isles and was written by David Talbot, who was then the club professional: "I would describe Holinwell – which is the popular name for the club – as a severe heathland type course: Played from the Championship tees it presents a formidable test for professionals and the top amateurs; the medal tees give a very interesting but slightly shorter course for the club competitions.

The best hole on the course is the 227-yard 14th, played from a high tee down a valley, at the foot of which is the green. The chief danger here is to underestimate the distance and be short."

Berkshire (Red)

THE BERKSHIRE GOLF CLUB
Swinley Road, Ascot, Berkshire, SL5 8AY, England
Telephone: +44 (0) 1344 621495
Website: None
Architect: Herbert Fowler
Visitors: By prior arrangement

Average Reviewers' Score

Reviewers' Comments

Great club, much friendlier than 'stuffy' Sunningdale... Wonderful course but it needs to be played more than once... The Red is definitely the better of the two courses, which are tough to spilt after the first visit... Both courses are great value and nobody I know who has played here has been disappointed... The Red is tighter and more intimate... Each hole is separated from the rest by the forest and each and every one of them is stunning... Many people claim that the Red and the Blue make up the finest 36-hole heathland combination in the world... The combination of six par threes, fours and fives is entertainment but it's the outstanding par threes which will stick in the mind...The par 3s are phenomenal... If you only have time for one round, make sure you play the Red rather than the Blue. The Red is a classic.

lany people say that there is nothing better than a day's golf amongst the forest, eather and springy turf of the Berkshire Golf Club. Both the Red and the Blue ɔurses are charming. The Red course is considered to be the more senior of the vo, but frankly there is little to choose between them.

erbert Fowler, who had a gift for blending golf courses into their natural ırroundings, laid out both courses in 1928. Fowler clearly did a great job ecause only minor changes have since been made to his original design. The land 'as once the hunting forest of the royals and dates back to the reign of Queen nne. Each hole is played in seclusion, the mature sycamore, birch, chestnut and ne trees providing majestic tunnels for the rippled fairways.

he Red acquired its name from a military analogy with the Blue taking the pposite side. The Red course is highly unusual in design. The configuration of six ır threes, six par fives and six par fours provide for much interest, variety and ıtertainment.

he Red's hallmark is most definitely e six par threes – they are all superb their own right. Actually, we think ıat this a fantastic golf course and will ovide a memorable day out for any rious golfer.

Paul Anderson – Head Professional writes:
I can't think of a better day's golfing than to play the Red and Blue courses at The Berkshire Golf Club. Just be careful not to eat too much lunch, otherwise you might not be able to appreciate the course in the afternoon!

Both courses are as wonderful as each other, with mature pine trees, heather and excellent greens combining to provide a picturesque yet testing day's golf.

dy Taylor

Royal Cinque Ports

ROYAL CINQUE PORTS GOLF CLUB
Golf Road, Deal, Kent, CT14 6RF, England
Telephone: +44 (0) 1304 374007
Website: www.royalcinqueports.com
Architect: Henry Hunter, James Braid, Sir Guy Campbell
Visitors: Contact in advance – Not Wed am or at weekend

Average Reviewers' Score:

Reviewers' Comments

A truly first class links... Tremendous history of Open Championships and Amateur Championships and its fearsome reputation is well deserved... New tees and bunker refurbishment have really improved this great course... If you want towering dunes and scenic beauty, forget Deal. However, those students of links golf who thrive on tight lies, rolling fairways, deep riveted bunkers and quick true greens will have a day to remember... Course is an hourglass in shape and the bit in the middle is quite dramatic with fairways and greens draped over the dunes... Front 9 isn't excessively long and it is here that you must try and make your score... From the 12th the stakes are raised and the homeward stretch is absolutely brutal... Links golf of the highest calibre and the 15th 16th and 17th wouldn't look out of place on any of the courses of the current Open Championship rota... Top class championship links golf at a reasonable price... Wow – links golf as it should be played... Would not hesitate to play it again... Wonderful!

Kevin Murray

oyal Cinque Ports, or Deal as it is more commonly known, is a brutal links ourse. Its back nine, or rather the last seven holes, are relentless, invariably aying directly into the teeth of the prevailing south westerly wind. The layout stark and cheerless – only the sandhills and wild dune grasses provide this arrow out-and-back layout with any real definition. You can expect tight and anging lies from the fairways, making stances awkward. Let's make no bones bout it – this is a tough course. Make your score on the front nine, otherwise eal can make even the very best golfers look like weekend duffers.

1909, J. H. Taylor – one of the Great Triumvirate – proudly won the first pen ever played at Royal Cinque orts. The Open returned to Deal in 920 and made Walter Hagen look ecidedly useless. In the lead-up to the pen, Hagen had boasted that he was nbeatable. He eventually ended up in 5th place!

920 was to be the last Open held at eal, despite the fact that it was planned return in 1949, but sadly the sea reached its defences and flooded the ourse.

Andrew Reynolds – Head Professional writes:
Deal is one of nature's masterpieces, as natural a course as you can find. Situated on an undulating stretch of sandhills, it follows the sea on its outward nine and when the holes reach our 'bottom end', you play straight back to the clubhouse.

This true links course is a severe battle – a shorter front nine with the testing back nine played into the prevailing wind. The giant slick greens will test the best and you will leave your day with an eager desire to return. Your memories will be of a course surrounded by the biggest sky and an even bigger test of your golf.

vin Murray

Rye (Old)

23

RYE GOLF CLUB
Camber, Rye, East Sussex, TN31 7QS, England
Telephone: +44 (0) 1797 225241
Website: www.ryegolfclub.co.uk
Architect: Harry Colt, Tom Simpson and Sir Guy Campbell
Visitors: By invitation only

Average Reviewers' Score

Reviewers' Comments

What an experience! Old-fashioned links as it was meant to be... Finally managed to play Rye after 12 years of trying and I have to say I was disappointed... One of the most interesting courses I have played in England... I always look forward to playing it, mainly because they have some of the finest links greens in the country but the course itself is a bit hit and miss... Proper links course, if you ever manage to get a tee time... Not as difficult to get on as they say, just contact them on their website in advance... Some of the par 4s are as tough as anywhere... 3, 4, and 13 were memorable... Traditional through and through, but somewhat spoilt on the turn with holes 10 and 11, which are more parkland-like and 17, which is a nothing hole... Courses don't have to be over 7,000 yards to be hard... Wonderful experience and well worth a visit... I would definitely play here again.

, we've arrived at Rye, but will we get a game? Well, Rye Golf Club is so very ivate that it is exceedingly difficult to secure a tee time. But wait a minute... the ub has recently launched a new website and many say it is now easier to get a me.

e was founded in 1894 and a young 25-year-old Harry Colt laid out the course surely one of the most impressive debut designs in history. Colt later became e's secretary. Today's layout bears the hallmark of Tom Simpson and Sir Guy ampbell, though the Second World War almost obliterated the links and a flying omb almost destroyed the clubhouse. But, thanks to the faithful few, Rye rose up e a phoenix.

ith a measly par of 68, and a course that measures over 6,300 yards, Rye has be one of the toughest courses in Britain. The one and only par five hits us raight away and it comes too early in the round to take too much advantage. ne five short holes are outstanding but brutal, with alarmingly elusive elevated eens. The remaining twelve par fours e there for the taking – well, three them at least. Nine others, yes nine, easure more than 400 yards in length.

Donald Steel writes:
My golfing daydreams revolve most frequently around Rye. There is a gentle breeze from the sea, the small boats with their coloured sails glide down past the harbour as the sun highlights the little town on its hill like a scene from fairyland.

No other course can stand comparison with it in terms of character, setting and atmosphere. Rye is Rye and that is the end of it.

e Brown

Worplesdon

WORPLESDON GOLF CLUB
Woking, Surrey, GU22 0RA, England
Telephone: +44 (0) 1483 472277
Website: www.worplesdongc.co.uk
Architect: John Abercromby
Visitors: Weekdays only - contact in advance

Average Reviewers' Score

Reviewers' Comments

I rate Worplesdon as one of the best, prettiest and most enjoyable courses I have played... Very enjoyable tree-lined heathland course with bags of visual appeal and the X-factor quality of a laid-back, relaxed club... Built over undulating heathland typical of this area, plenty of heather and trees if you stray off line... 1st is one of the most impressive starting holes I have played – a lovely raised tee to the left of the pro shop looks down on a beautiful fairway... Good variety from hole to hole... Par 3s are amongst the best... Par 5s should flatter your golf... Good driving is rewarded... Signature hole is the 10th over a lake... Last three holes are tough and par is hard to achieve on each... Walking off the 18th, though, I felt very pleased with myself... Club maintains the traditions of the game and its beautiful sleepy clubhouse, with its wood panelling and gabled roofs, epitomises the very essence of Surrey heathland golf... Thoroughly recommended.

Andy Taylor

Vorplesdon is one of the prettiest and most delightful of Surrey's many heath ıd heather courses and it's arguably the best of the trinity of "Ws" (West Hill ıd Woking being the other two); all three courses virtually border each other. is set amongst glorious heather, chestnut and pine trees. John Abercromby's augural design dates back to 1908 and little has changed after almost 100 years.

's not a long course at just less than 6,500 yards, but it's supremely challenging ıd driving accuracy is far more important than length. The front nine plays :ross stunning undulating terrain, so expect some awkward stances. The ack nine is sited on relatively even ground. The greens are always in fabulous ondition and are lightning fast with some subtle borrows and undulations. The ne-shotters are especially strong and the 175-yard 13th is an absolute cracker, ırrounded by bunkers and often rated as one of the best par threes in the UK.

's a real privilege to play this quiet and elegant course where the springy irways roll gently up and down, flanked by many mature trees. The profusion f heather provides stunning seasonal colour and a real challenge in finding the ayward golf ball. The clubhouse is one f the most pleasant in all the land and ery welcoming.

The following passage was published in Henry Cotton's Guide to Golf In The British Isles and was written by Alan Waters who was then the club professional:
"Worplesdon is one of the heather and pine-type courses found throughout Surrey, not a long course by some standards, but one which demands accuåracy. Our greens have only slight borrows and are very true and not too tricky."

ıdy Taylor

Woburn (Duke's)

WOBURN GOLF & COUNTRY CLUB
Little Brickhill, Milton Keynes, Bucks, MK17 9LJ, England
Telephone: +44 (0) 1908 370756
Website: www.golf.discoverwoburn.co.uk
Architect: Charles Lawrie
Visitors: Contact in advance – midweek only

Average Reviewers' Score:

Reviewers' Comments

What a joy! Can't really think you could want much more from a course... Although the Duke's is a great course, I think it is the weakest of the three here at Woburn, but having said that, I think it has the best greens. They are huge, tricky to read and, in the summer, as fast as lightning... Lovely layout, great challenge and good condition... Course wasn't in very good condition when I played it... First four holes are absolutely superb, but after that, the rest seem rather samey... There's something a bit ordinary about some of the holes, although all the par threes are good... Some good par 3s... Memorable holes include the 4th and the 13th, the latter has a really tough approach across a ravine to a tight green... Overall an excellent course, but the Duchess would be my first choice any day... I would heartily recommend the Duke's to anyone whether scratch or 18... Give it a try.

elevision has turned Woburn into one of the best-known golfing venues in ritain. But in the scheme of things, golf here is still in its infancy. On the other and, the famous Woburn Abbey has been home to the Bedford family for almost 00 years.

was Lord Tavistock's brilliant idea to bring golf to Woburn. He commissioned harles Lawrie of Cotton & Pennink, to design the Duke's. After two years, and uch tree-felling, the first course at Woburn opened for play. With fairways anked by glorious pine, birch and hestnut trees, the Duke's is an intimate olf course. Each hole is played in olendid isolation. It's a serious challenge o, measuring almost 7,000 yards from e back tees and 6,550 from the regular es. Straight and long driving is the rder of the day. This is not a course for e novice golfer – it will beat you up nd spit you out.

here are some fantastic holes on e Duke's but the pick of the bunch the famous par three 3rd. Framed y rhododendrons and gorse, this is a enuinely delightful golf hole. The green 100 feet below the tee, and the hard reen slopes violently from back to ont. Measuring only 125 yards, a short on must be played to the heart of the reen, otherwise the ball is likely to cuttle off, pronto.

Alistair Tait writes:
Stand on the first tee of the Duke's Course at Woburn and it's hard to believe this magnificent layout has only been in existence since 1976. It has an old world feel of maturity and tradition, as if it has been around since the early 1900s.

Mature pine trees, silver birch, chestnut and magnificent banks of rhododendron bushes provide a splendid backdrop to a course that is among the best inland tracks in all of Europe. No sooner had the Duke's opened for play than Europe's best golfers were putting it to the test. Three years after opening, the course hosted the 1979 Dunlop Masters. Australian Graham Marsh won the title that year. Two years later Greg Norman made it an antipodean double by adding his own name to the trophy.

WEST SUSSEX GOLF CLUB

Average Reviewers' Score:

Golf Club Lane, Wiggonholt, Pulborough, West Sussex
RH20 2EN, England
Telephone: +44 (0) 1798 872426 **Website:** www.westsussexgolf.co.uk
Architect: Sir Guy Campbell and Major C. K. Hutchinson
Visitors: Contact in advance – Not Tue am or Fri all day

Reviewers' Comments

One of the unsung English gems... Marvellous, traditional and a quintessential English clu with plus-fours, three-hour rounds and foursomes – just how golf used to be played... Totally beautiful, traditional and a thoroughly enjoyable test of golf... It's the real thing and there's nothing much better for me anywhere in the world... Thoroughly enjoyed my round on the pure heathland layout... Hard to imagine a better course... Its difficulty definitely belies the Par 68... What it lacks in length is more than made up by strategic placement of heather and bunkers (especially on the doglegs)... Scoring on this dream course is not easy... Was impressed by the renowned 6th but also the long par 3 12th... Par 3s are brilliant and the course has a really strong finish... The gentle opener is the only easy birdie opportunity... Classic heathland course... It won't test the tour pros bu it will put a smile on every handicap golfer's face... Anyone who has not played here is missing a complete treat.

Ve make no apology for declaring that West Sussex Golf Club is one of our avourite inland courses. It is sheer delight to play golf on this charming sandy utcrop of heathland. The course occupies a priceless, stunning, undulating site on he northern edge of the South Downs.

the scheme of things, West Sussex is a relative youngster, dating back to 1930. ir Guy Campbell and Major C K Hutchinson designed the course and these two rchitects created one of the most natural and aesthetically pleasing golf courses England.

On the surface of it, West Sussex is a short course, measuring 6,200 yards from he back tees, but you will do very well to play to your handicap and it's unlikely hat you will get the impression that the course is short. Clearly, this isn't a hampionship course but it will provide a challenging and thought-provoking ound for the very best golfers whilst remaining enjoyable for the higher andicapper.

he holes wind their way through enchanting woodland, with oak, silver birch nd pine providing a pretty backdrop and the heather and the cunning bunkering roviding the definition. The colours, especially in autumn, are breathtaking. Each ole demands thought and holds attention, there is a great deal of variation to he holes and many are memorable.

here isn't a signature hole as such, but ve especially like the 6th, a 224-yard ownhill par three with a pond lurking 0 yards in front of the green; to make natters worse, the whole area of pond out-of-bounds.

Bernard Darwin writes:
The day on which to see Pulborough, if not to play our best on it, is one when the wind is blowing hard, for the sand is wafted in great puffs, like white clouds across the course, so that we can scarcely believe that the sea is not round the corner.

HUNSTANTON GOLF CLUB

Golf Course Road, Old Hunstanton, Norfolk, PE36 6JQ, England
Telephone: +44 (0) 1485 532811
Website: www.club-noticeboard.co.uk/hunstanton/
Architect: George Fernie, James Braid, James Sherlock
Visitors: Contact in advance – must be a golf club member – not weekends

Average Reviewers' Score

Reviewers' Comments

A classic links up-and-back course, with several intriguing holes and no poor ones... Total entertainment... We played on a glorious May afternoon with only a 1-club wind, so some of the course's defences were removed. But there are enough tough bunkers to concentrate the mind, especially on the enjoyable par 3s... Have played here on numerous occasions and the greens are consistently fast and true... Greens weren't as fast as many have suggested, but they ran true and were in good condition... Greens second to none... Superb undulating fairways... I had not played for 7/8 years and the course was not as I remember it. The fairways now have water on them and are not like links fairways at all... Couple of blind shots... Not the most challenging links I have ever played but still worth every penny... Back at the clubhouse the bar food was excellent and the members and staff very friendly and welcoming... The course is good honest fun... Definitely recommended.

unstanton is a natural course and a simple out and back affair, interrupted only
riefly in the middle of the outward and inward nines by a few short holes that
gzag at right angles across the central dunes. The River Hun and the Wash frame
is narrow strip of links land, but you are only offered a few glimpses of the sea
om the course itself.

unstanton and Royal West Norfolk are near neighbours and both courses
re usually rated similarly in the ranking tables. Hunstanton is certainly a
onnoisseur's golf course, jammed full of memorable quality golf holes and the
embers are quite rightly proud of the greens, which are tricky to read, fast, hard
nd true. The rippling fairways are tightly mown and gently undulating.

wo of the world's best lady golfers have played and won here at Hunstanton. In
e year before the Great War, Cecil Leitch beat G Ravenscroft 2 and 1 to win
e Ladies' British Amateur Championship and in 1921, the great Joyce Wethered
eat J Stocker to win the English Ladies' Close Amateur Championship. More
ecently, in 1972, Hunstanton hosted the Ladies' British Amateur Championship;
hen Mickey Walker went on to win, beating Claudine Rubin of France.

feat of incalculable odds also occurred at Hunstanton. In 1974, the amateur
ob Taylor holed in one during a practice round for the Eastern Counties
oursomes. The following day, in the actual competition, he again holed in one.
he very next day in the same competition, he once more holed in one. If a hole
one on three consecutive days is not enough, you'll be amazed to hear that it
as achieved each time on the same hole, the 16th, a 191-yard par three!

unstanton is a tough, full-blown championship golf links; an absolute must-play
r serious golfers. Make your score on the outward nine, the back nine is much
ore difficult, except for the par three 16th, a simple hole in one opportunity.

Belfry (Brabazon)

THE BELFRY
Wishaw, North Warwickshire, B76 9PR, England
Telephone: +44 (0) 1675 470301
Website: www.thebelfry.com
Architect: Peter Alliss and Dave Thomas
Visitors: Welcome – book in advance

Average Reviewers' Score.

Reviewers' Comments

Blown away by the condition and the whole experience… An absolute must-play course, a bit pricey, but an unforgettable experience… Thought it was really good and got a good deal too… Loads better than I thought… Great feeling when playing the 10th and 18th… Fame for fame's sake… Look past the Ryder Cup excitement and you will find a fairly ordinary course. Ordinary, that is, apart from the feature holes, the 10th and 18th… Some of the other holes are fine too and the course has matured loads since I was last there watching the Ryder Cups… Course has far more thrills than just the 10th and 18th alone – for example, the 17th is fantastic… Really enjoyed my game here and I loved everything about it… Course is very strategic and has a very strong run of holes at the end… Not the prettiest place to be but it is a good well-maintained course with a great history… A superb course and a great facility.

ne Brabazon course at The Belfry doesn't need introducing. After all, it's unique. nis course has played host to more Ryder Cups than any other course on the anet - four in total. The excitement comes from playing memorable and familiar oles. And, following Dave Thomas's £2.7m makeover in the late 90s, there is ore water on The Brabazon than just about any other inland course in the ritish Isles – take a few extra balls.

vo outstanding holes have been opularised by television – the 10th and 3th. The former is a unique short par ur with water running along the right and side of the fairway. It is driveable you've seen Seve do it – so go on, ou've got to go for it! The closing ole is also dramatic and dominated by ater. It rewards the brave. Cut off as uch of the water as you can from the e, and you will be left with a shorter pproach shot, which must carry a lake n its way to a long, narrow, triple-tiered een. This hole has seen more Ryder up emotion than any other hole in the orld. For this reason alone, to follow in ne footsteps of golf's greatest legends, he Brabazon is a must-play course.

Gary Silcock – Head of Golf writes:
So much more than four Ryder Cups, 30 years of golfing giants treading its fairways and two of the most famous holes in golf, every hole of The Brabazon course will offer you an unforgettable challenge.

From the choice of four tee grounds, navigate the winding fairways flanked by myriad specimen deciduous and evergreen trees. Whilst negotiating the skilfully sculptured bunkers and the environmentally exquisite water hazards that tease twelve of the holes, take a moment to feel the presence of the Ryder Cup legends whose footsteps you are about to follow.

Make your own magic by driving the 10th like Seve, or rattling the cup on the 18th's three tiered green looking up at the world-famous ivory building.

ALWOODLEY GOLF CLUB
Wigton Lane, Leeds, Yorkshire, LS17 8SA, England
Telephone: +44 (0) 113 268 1680
Website: www.alwoodley.co.uk
Architect: Alister MacKenzie and Harry Colt
Visitors: Contact secretary in advance

Average Reviewers' Score

Reviewers' Comments

Alwoodley is absolutely fantastic from start to finish... Top quality course, which is playable all year round... Have played a number of times and walked round for Open Qualifying and it's a breathtaking heathland experience... Only Ganton can better this course in Yorkshire... Fantastic MacKenzie layout mixing a series of challenging 4s, long and short 3s and super 5s all flanked by heather and gorse... Distances are tough to judge, even with a yardage chart... Cross the road after the short but tricky 2nd and walk onto golfing heaven... It's a tough no-frills heathland/moorland test and it's always a delight to play here... A golfer's golf course... You'll need to have your swing intact if you plan to score well... Grand isolation as you play and golf of the finest quality... Clubhouse is very unusual... Simply tremendous and I can't wait to return to try and improve on my last feeble score... If I lived in or around Leeds, this is where I'd want to play... Stunning.

VirtualCaddy.co.uk

lwoodley is certainly one of the finest and most subtle inland courses in the ·itish Isles, located in a secluded spot. "This the home course of Dr. Mackenzie ıght to be good and, personally, I put it very high among inland courses." Wrote ernard Darwin in his book The Golf Courses of Great Britain.

ounded in 1907, Alwoodley is the cream of a cluster of excellent courses retching across the moors just north of Leeds. The great Alister Mackenzie (a octor at the time) joined forces with the already renowned architect, Harry olt, to fashion Alwoodley. This was Dr Mackenzie's first dabble with golf course esign. Clearly inspired, he went on to become a full time golf course architect id later went on to design the great Augusta National, home of the Masters.

ıe course is a combination of heathland and moorland with rippling fairways id fine, crisp, springy turf. There is plenty of heather and gorse, which provides orious seasonal colour and punishes the wayward shot. There are few trees, her than the occasional cluster of pines and silver birches on this glorious, indswept heath.

ssentially an out and back course, the front nine is generally regarded as the sier of the two nines (the only two par fives are on the outward nine). The ıck nine invariably plays into the prevailing winds coming off the Yorkshire oors.

ake sure that you bring your full compliment of golf clubs. It is likely that this ırd but fair course will force you to use every club in the bag. Alwoodley has ayed host to many important amateur events over the years and it regularly sts the pros when the course is used as a Regional Qualifier for the Open.

ın C Birch - Alwoodley Golf Club

Hankley Common

HANKLEY COMMON GOLF CLUB
Tilford, Farnham, Surrey, GU10 2DD, England
Telephone: +44 (0) 1252 792493
Website: www.hankley.co.uk
Architect: James Braid, Harry Colt
Visitors: Weekdays and pm at weekends

Average Reviewers' Score

Reviewers' Comments

Simply the best and most enjoyable heathland golf course... This golf course is just gorgeous; it oozes quality, history and class... A Colt/Braid classic... Design is fantastic.. From the minute your starter directs your drive towards a green in the distance, with heather in flower down both sides of the fairways, you know you're playing a great course... A tranquil space that offers every kind of shot the game has to offer... Some holes are tight in places and finding the fairway is a must... Course races off to a difficul start then settles down with some shortish par 4s... It really gets going from the 6th... 7th rated quite rightly as one of the greatest par 3s in GB&I... Holes around the turn are particularly good... Feeling of space whilst surrounded by miles of purple heather makes a visual treat... Most noticeable improvements are off the course, gone is the old stuffiness... Played 36 and would have gone round again... Courses like this are few and far between.

Christopher O'Neil-Dunne

ınkley Common is situated on the North Downs, in a preservation area or be precise, a 'Site of Special Scientific Interest', home to oak, rowan and the ɔodlark. The common at Tilford has ferocious heather and a wide-open and ndswept appearance. If there was ever a place where seaside links golf meets and heathery golf, it's here at Hankley Common.

ıere is an overwhelming feeling of spaciousness on this heathland course, much so that it seems plausible that a second or third course could be :ertwined between the existing 18 holes. To put everything into context, the urse occupies 164 acres, but the club actually owns more than 850 acres perfect heathland. Don't let this feeling of space lull you into a false sense security – this is not the place to open your shoulders and let rip. Anything ghtly off-line will be swallowed up by bunkers, or even worse, by the thick ngled heather.

ght new back tees are now in play, adding more than 250 extra yards. Hankley ommon now measures an impressive 702 yards from the tips. This is a really chnically testing golf course. Regional ualifying for the Open has been held Hankley Common since 1984 and e club has hosted numerous other ıportant amateur and professional ents over the years.

ɔ, if you are looking for a memorable, sting and underrated golf course with ıtstanding greens, look no further than ankley Common.

Peter Stow – Professional writes:
Hankley Common is an outstanding example of heathland golf. It has a links-like feel and is a true test for golfers of all standards.

It was originally modelled by James Braid and added to by Harry Colt in 1936. The course has retained all its character and the addition of purple tees have given the course additional length that is an undoubtedly a requirement of today's golfer.

chelle Baxter

BEARWOOD LAKES GOLF CLUB
Bearwood Road, Sindlesham, Nr. Wokingham, Berkshire, RG41 4SJ
Telephone: +44 (0) 118 979 7900
Website: www.bearwoodlakes.co.uk
Architect: Martin Hawtree
Visitors: Only as member's guest

Average Reviewers' Score

Reviewers' Comments

Possibly the most beautiful course that I have played… Mature beyond its years… Exquisitely designed course that takes full advantage of the natural landscape and surroundings – an intoxicating blend of heath, forest and lake… Layout is through woodland with stands of pine trees defining many holes… Holes dogleg right and left, there are uphill and downhill holes, and holes where a birdie is a real possibility and others where a par is a great relief… Superbly designed with the varied holes going in all directions… Long straight hitting over water is a requirement on a number of holes… Variety makes this a great course… It's a very thorough test – you will need brains and also brawn… Greens are like glass in the summer… Very well bunkered, with lightning fast greens... Practice facilities and clubhouse are also excellent… One of the best courses anywhere for standard of playing conditions and welcome… Most underrated course in the area… World-class… If you can get on, you won't be disappointed.

Bearwood Lakes Golf Club

ıe course at Bearwood Lakes Golf Club first opened for play in 1996 and artin Hawtree designed a thrilling course, which wends its way through the ature trees of the former Bearwood Estate. It looks mature beyond its years ıd is certainly one of the very best new courses to have been built in the last n years.

awtree has skilfully blended the course into the natural surroundings and the :autiful specimen trees add to the any attractive features. There isn't a ıgle weak hole – each and every one akes you think. The most memorable ›les are the six sited around the ıtural lakes, which cover more than) acres. To score well, especially from e back tees, you'll need to bring your ' game. The fairways are relatively :nerous in terms of width but if you ray off this carpeted surface, you'll be trouble.

:arwood Lakes is not the most :cessible course. You'll need to abduct member to get a game here. But if you › manage to get on, you will be totally :lighted, because this is a course for ıe connoisseur.

David Newling Ward – Chairman writes:

"The moment that I first saw the Bearwood Estate, I knew that it had the potential to become one of Britain's finest golf courses. I am delighted to say that my vision has now become a reality.

A golf club, no matter how good the greens, fairways and the clubhouse, is not a true club without its members and the ambience they create. We are fortunate to have an enthusiastic and friendly membership who make the most of the many competitions and matches that take place throughout the year. At Bearwood Lakes the enjoyment of our members and their guests is our prime concern. I very much look forward to welcoming you personally to Bearwood Lakes, should you become a member."

ɜrwood Lakes Golf Club

WOBURN GOLF & COUNTRY CLUB
Little Brickhill, Milton Keynes, Bucks, MK17 9LJ, England
Telephone: +44 (0) 1908 370756
Website: www.golf.discoverwoburn.co.uk
Architect: Ross McMurray, Clive Clark, Peter Alliss and Alex Hay
Visitors: Contact in advance – midweek only

Average Reviewers' Score

Reviewers' Comments

Woburn's third and newest course is like the more familiar Duke's and Duchess but on steroids... Everything is a little bigger, greens are bigger, fairways wider and course longer... A more open challenge than its neighbours but well bunkered and with no blin drives... Undulating fairways, shaped greens and no repetition... 7th is an excellent big boy's hole but there are a few others which are likely to bamboozle you... Finishing fou holes will test your long irons... Plenty to challenge the low handicapper... There are two main weaknesses, first is the par 3s, they are fairly nondescript and second is the fac that you can hit driver on most of the par 4s and 5s and get away with it... Great for the golfer who likes to be tested but not battered into submission... Will return happily to play the Marquess again... Make sure you take in the "Woburn Carvery" as this is something to behold... Deserves to be higher in the rankings, it has the potential to be the Top 10.

ıe addition of the new Marquess course at Woburn Golf and Country Club puts 'oburn in a unique position, standing out on its own as the only venue to have three ›urses ranked in the Top 100.

ıe Marquess course straddles the county boundary of Bedfordshire and ıckinghamshire and is set within 200 acres of majestic mature woodland, part of the :lightful 3,000-acre Woburn Abbey Estate.

took a quartet of architects to develop e Marquess: Ross McMurray, Clive Clark, :ter Alliss and Alex Hay, the course ›ening for play in 1999. The Marquess is fferent in nature to the Duke's and the uchess, but perfectly complementary. ıirways are wider and the land more ndulating. Trees are more park-like, aturing oak, yew, chestnut, rowan and :ech, whereas the other two courses are 'edominantly carved through pine forests.

's a supremely challenging golf course, easuring well over 7,000 yards from the ıck tees. In 2001 and 2002, it stole the ritish Masters from its elder brother, the uke's. There is absolutely no doubt that /oburn is a classy place to play golf and ›w, with three superb golf courses, it is ne of the most desirable golfing venues in ngland.

Alistair Tait writes:
Few new courses in recent times have captured the headlines in the way the new Marquess course at Woburn has. Fewer still have been ready to test Europe's top golfers so soon after construction. The Marquess had achieved both feats within just a year of construction.

Europe's elite were sceptical when the Victor Chandler British Masters was switched from the long established and much loved Duke's course to the Marquess for the 2001 tournament. Yet all it took was one practice round for the professionals to agree the Marquess was a fantastic addition to the Woburn Golf & Country Club. Former European number one Colin Montgomerie came off the course after his first practice round and proclaimed: "This is a great course and it has got my name on it. It is perfect for my game."

THE GROVE
Chandler's Cross, Hertfordshire, WD3 4TG
Telephone: +44 (0) 1923 294266
Website: www.thegrove.co.uk
Architect: Kyle Phillips
Visitors: Welcome – book in advance

Average Reviewers' Score

Reviewers' Comments

Stunning new course... Well prepared and in excellent condition... Kyle Phillips has worked a minor miracle with ordinary land... Conditioning is faultless and the service is second to none... Fairways were the best I have experienced in the UK and the greens were lightning fast... Have played it a couple of times now and each time becomes more enjoyable as you work out the do's and definitely don'ts of the course... Overrated, overpriced, overplayed... Having played here in January, I cannot praise this place high enough... Plenty of good-looking holes with undulating fairways and pot bunkers waiting to snare wayward drives... The design, like Kingsbarns, is subtle but the greens and bunkering are first rate... One of the best winter courses around... It's the rising star of UK golf courses... This place is aimed at the wealthy rather than the normal punter... Fantastic course and so close to London... You must go at least once... From parking up to going home, this place is pure golf heaven.

he Grove is one of the newest and most enterprising golf course projects in the ritish Isles. Designed by Kyle Phillips (the man behind Kingsbarns), the course pened for play in September 2003 to rave reviews and it's already considered by ome to be the best course inside the 125. This is not your typical golf club. In ct, it isn't a golf club at all – it's a pay-nd-play golf course open to everyone.

hillips has done a neat job, using the atural contours of the land in an nderstated way to create a discerning ourse. Four large teeing areas on each nd every hole cater for all golfing andards. Measuring a hefty 7,150 yards om the back tees to a leisurely 5,500 ards from the front tees. The raised ndulating greens are simply fantastic, ery fast and very true. There are no xcuses for three putting here. However, you miss the green with your approach hot, you can be faced with some very icky recovery chip shots.
he Grove is certainly a course for the ognoscenti.

Spencer Schaub – Director of Golf writes:
Located on the outskirts of London, The Grove is a jewel of golf course design and five star service. Opened in September 2003, the Kyle Phillips designed course has already hosted the World Golf Championships American Express Championship, and was described by the best players in the world as the greatest conditioned golf course they play in Europe. The course is generously spread over 200 acres around the impressive Victorian mansion, with the first half being a stern test of long iron approaches and deep bunkers and the back nine demanding finesse as it winds through wooded areas.

One of the finest courses in Europe, The Grove gives all players the chance to tread in Tiger's footsteps and experience quality of playing areas and service, in a fantastically relaxed atmosphere. Distinctly different from any other golfing facilities.

MOORTOWN GOLF CLUB
Harrogate Road, Leeds, LS17 7DB
Telephone: +44 (0) 113 268 6521
Website: www.moortown-gc.co.uk
Architect: Dr Alister MacKenzie
Visitors: Contact in advance

Average Reviewers' Score

Reviewers' Comments

Moortown is a truly excellent day out… Worth playing for just one hole, the 10th, Gibraltar, it's a simply fantastic par three… 10th and 18th holes are exceptional… You are presented with a variety of challenges and all aspects of your game need to be in order if you are to play to your handicap… Low handicappers welcomed to play from the back tees… Varied and interesting layout that provides a testing challenge… Overall presentation was superb… Excellent greens, lots of tradition and very welcoming… Friendly welcome and a great test of golf… It's a great course with plenty of history. Moortown has it all.

ɔortown Golf Club is classic ɔorland golf course with ⁄ely peaty turf that provides e bouncy cushion-effect when ılking – a course that is gentle ı the feet. The fairways appear de and inviting – many of the ıles are flanked with silver birch, rse and heather. But don't be ɔled, Moortown is no pushover. ıis golf course is tough and acting.

turned out to be a tough test r Walter Hagen, the 1929 Ryder ıp captain and his American am. For it was here, at a cold ɔortown, that Great Britain and eland, with George Duncan as ptain, beat the USA 7-5. This as the first Ryder Cup to be ld on home soil.

ıe holes offer a great deal of riety, both in terms of look d feel and in shot-making quirements and as always with acKenzie's design, Moortown fits e land like a glove.

Martin Heggie – Advanced PGA Professional writes:

Moortown has always held a richly deserved reputation as one of the country's finest championship golf courses… tough but fair, a blend of perfect moorland turf, immaculate greens, natural hazards of gorse, heather, woodland and streams.

From the opening par five there are many fine holes to enjoy including the new 6th, rated the most difficult, and the famous Gibraltar par three 10th with its sloping plateau green, the club's signature hole. Typical of all great courses, there is a classic finish. With its fairway favouring strategically placed bunkers, the 18th requires two exceptional shots to find the well-guarded green which nestles under the clubhouse windows.

Many famous shots have been played at Moortown's 18th hole. Severiano Ballesteros once managed to fly a nine-iron approach shot clean over the green to the practice putting green! The most historic shot of all was that of Nigel Denham during the English Stroke Play Championship. His approach shot missed the green and entered the clubhouse, from where a window was opened and he was allowed to play his shot back onto the green. This is no longer possible… the clubhouse is now out of bounds.

Chart Hills

CHART HILLS GOLF CLUB *Average Reviewers' Score*
Weeks Lane, Biddenden, Kent, TN27 8JX, England
Telephone: +44 (0) 1580 292222
Website: www.charthills.co.uk
Architect: Nick Faldo and Steve Smyers
Visitors: Welcome – after 1pm Mon, Wed, Sat, Sun and before 1pm Fri

Reviewers' Comments

Thank you Mr. Faldo! One of the best new inland courses… Has the feel of a seaside links when the wind blows… Visually and technically intimidating course winding through this beautiful Kent valley… Layout is a real strategist's delight with many shot options presented on every hole and no real benefit to the long hitter except on a couple of holes… Vast amount of bunkers (138 of them) are a key factor but the variety of holes for me is the biggest plus point… Remember your sand wedge, you will go in at least one bunker… Requires the full repertoire of shot making… Numerous challenges, particularly the 'risk and reward' Par 4s and 5s… Only surprise was the Par 3s, which apart from 17 are truly forgettable… Too many great holes to mention but the one for me is 17. Think Florida, think Sawgrass, think island green. Any shot short, left, right or long is wet, simple as that… In every way Chart Hills could be one of the best courses in the country.

ıart Hills is set in the peaceful rural heart of the Garden of England where old k trees stand guard and where there is sand, lots and lots of sand.

ıis is Nick Faldo's first European design and the discerning American designer, eve Smyers, supported him, opening for play in 1993. They have created a big d attractive golf course with acres of water and sand to trip up the very best lfers.

ıe design is bold and uses the natural contours of the land to good effect. ıe fairways twist and turn in every conceivable direction, heading towards the ıge and frighteningly undulating greens. ıe bunkering is daring in the extreme, travagant and exceptionally varied, nging from small deep pot bunkers to e huge serpent-like "Anaconda" bunker ı the par five 5th that wiggles along r more than 200 yards. Water hazards ıture extensively at Chart Hills. These, o, come in all shapes and sizes and are :quently in play, especially on the short r three 17th where the green is an and.

round of golf at Chart Hills is a emorable experience. The course is ways immaculately maintained and e variety of the holes will keep you oroughly entertained from your first ive to your last putt.

James Cornish – Director of Golf writes:
Chart Hills is set in what was centuries ago the dense 'Andredsweald Forest.' I feel very privileged to be the Director of Golf at my favourite course in the South East.

The famous greens are very large, fast and undulating. In my view therein lies the challenge of Nick Faldo's design. The fairways are often generous but to have a putt from below the hole the golfer must be approaching the green from the correct area of the fairway. Get on the wrong side of the pin and a three putt is likely. The course demands a strong all round game but affords players of all abilities the chance to enjoy their visit.

ALDEBURGH GOLF CLUB

Saxmundham Road, Aldeburgh, Suffolk, IP15 5PE
Telephone: +44 (0) 1728 452890
Website: www.aldeburghgolfclub.co.uk
Architect: John Thompson, Willie Fernie, Willie Park Jnr. & J. H. Taylor
Visitors: Contact in advance

Average Reviewers' Scor

Reviewers' Comments

Aldeburgh is a riot of colour in the summer… With a par of 68 and SSS of 71, this is one of the most difficult courses in the region… Played here with a friend who's a 28 handicapper, he found too much gorse and nearly killed himself twice when he thinned h ball into the sleeper-faced bunkers! Its sandy soil means that it plays beautifully 52 week per year… Great par fours– tough to play to handicap… If you can keep on the straight and narrow, Aldeburgh is there for the taking, but if you are wayward you are in for a prickly time… Very enjoyable and in excellent condition, deserves to be higher in the rankings… Excellent greens… two balls only means that rounds are quick (we played a round in three hours)… Would love to go back here in the early summer and once mor experience the gorse in flower… Didn't have my camera the last time I played, I won't forget it next time!

ɔunded in 1884, Aldeburgh is one of the oldest golf courses in Suffolk and is ꞉parated from the tidal Alde estuary by an unusual strip of maritime heathland. lthough the course itself is ostensibly heathland, its close proximity to the ꞉tuary and the North Sea provides a salty whiff of sea air.

was originally designed by John Thompson and Willie Fernie and modified the turn of the 20th century by Willie Park Jnr. and J.H.Taylor. Benjamin ritten once lived close to the course, bringing fame to the town through the ternationally renowned music festivals at Snape Maltings.

you play Aldeburgh between May and late June, you will be presented with eautiful narrow fairways weaving their way between bright yellow gorse. You ill be hard-pressed to find such an awe-inspiring sight at any golf course. learly, you need to be on top of your game. Looking for golf balls in this terrain a painful business. "I am also very fond of Aldeburgh," wrote Darwin, "though ɔw and again when I am sore and spiky from sitting in gorse bushes, and hot and red from searching for my ball, I could wish there was just a little less gorse."

eep, sleeper-faced bunkers protect ɔme of the greens. Combine this with ie ever-changing wind and you are resented with an excellent golfing hallenge. Or as Darwin said: "I know o course more likely to teach driving ccuracy. There is nearly always a wind n that most pleasant heath, and there re very often avenues of gorse, and you mply must keep straight."

Sir Peter Allen writes:
The most conspicuous feature here is the brilliance of the yellow gorse which in its full flowering season almost dazzles the eyes with its golden masses of flowers. The brilliant yellow gorse of East Anglia was said to have been the inspiration of the colour scheme for the engines of the long gone Midland and Great Northern Join Railway.

THE BERKSHIRE GOLF CLUB
Swinley Road, Ascot, Berkshire, SL5 8AY, England
Telephone: +44 (0) 1344 621495
Website: None
Architect: Herbert Fowler
Visitors: By prior arrangement

Average Reviewers' Score

Reviewers' Comments

Can safely say that the Blue is a truly stunning course... The Blue is every bit as good as the Red with the same excellent tee to green conditioning... It's much more of a conventional layout than the Red with four par3s, three par 5s and the rest fours... Not the easiest opener after lunch and a couple of beers... From the par3 start to the tough par 4 finishing hole, this was a great all-round test with many long carries from the tee... The Blue has a more open feel to it and it's certainly more forgiving than the Red... One of the most endearing features of both courses is the variation of each hole so you are forever on your toes... It's traditional and friendly and they serve one of the best lunches I've ever tasted... The Berkshire is a wonderful club and if I could be a member, I'd jump at the chance as they do everything right.

Andy Taylor

ıe Blue course at The Berkshire Golf Club is the Red's more conventional and ghtly shorter sister. A more standard four par 3s, three par 5s and eleven par 4s ake up the configuration for this delightful par 71 course.

erbert Fowler was the Berkshire's architect and the Blue course opened for ay in 1928. Fowler was actually very good at designing excellent twin golf ›urses. Not only did Fowler design both courses here at the Berkshire, but he so designed the superb intertwined courses at Walton Heath, the Old and the ew.

›th the Berkshire courses have the same natural hazards, although the Blue ays over flatter ground than the Red. Cruelly, the Blue opens up with an ceptionally tough par 3, with the tee directly in front of the clubhouse window. ıe green sits on a distant plateau. Not the easiest hole on which to start a und of golf – play the Red course in the morning to prepare for it!
ıere are many other notable holes on the Blue course but it's the closing quence of five holes that makes this tough but special course. All five are ır 4s and three of them are more an 400 yards long.

Paul Anderson – Head Professional writes:
I can't think of a better day's golfing than to play the Red and Blue courses at The Berkshire Golf Club. Just be careful not to eat too much lunch, otherwise you might not be able to appreciate the course in the afternoon!

Both courses are as wonderful as each other, with mature pine trees, heather and excellent greens combining to provide a picturesque yet testing day's golf.

dy Taylor

West Hill

WEST HILL GOLF CLUB
Bagshot Road, Brookwood, Surrey, GU24 0BH, England
Telephone: +44 (0) 1483 474365
Website: www.westhill-golfclub.co.uk
Architect: Cuthbert Butchart
Visitors: Contact secretary in advance

Average Reviewers' Scor

Reviewers' Comments

West Hill is a fantastic course that maybe does not get the recognition it deserves... It is comparable to the East at Wentworth but surpasses it when it comes to VFM... Whil not long in distance, it requires a lot of careful planning off the tee and approaches must be very accurate, as you can ill afford to be above the hole... Not the hardest course in the world, but is nicely designed and very enjoyable... Only two par 5s, which means any birdies must be found on difficult par 4s and dangerous par 3s... Great par 3s (som of the best I have seen and all on one course) and a good mix of par 4s ensure that the course is a pleasure to play... Should be on everyone's must-play list... Two of England's finest courses are almost next to each other... If you are ever on the M3 leave at junction 3 and go and play it. You can always tell the wife you were stuck on the M25!

Kevin Murray

'est Hill is the youngest of the trinity of "Ws" located in this most beautiful rner of Surrey (Woking and Worplesdon being the other two). The course is uted in an out and back fashion across undulating sandy ground. The fairways e lined with pine, birch and, of course, tangly heather. Measuring slightly more an 6,350 yards, West Hill is not long by day's standards, but with only two par 'es and a lowly par of 69, it represents enjoyable and testing challenge.

ıe key to scoring well at West Hill is e successful negotiation of the five ort holes and the best of these is ıdoubtedly the 15th, which measures 2 yards from the back tees. British lf luminary Henry Cotton felt that the 5th was one of the best short holes in 'itain and, for a while, Cotton shared e West Hill course record with a 67.

it's charm that you are looking for, en you need look no further than /est Hill. This is a truly delightful golf ɔurse.

Guy Shoesmith – Professional writes:
West Hill is truly one of Surrey's oldest gems. It is a heathland course, designed in 1907, lined with towering Scots pines and featuring the brook of Brookwood, which meanders its way through the course, coming into play on six different holes.

In late spring, the course is ablaze with the colour of rhododendrons in full bloom and in late summer, the flowering heather becomes a sea of purple, which requires carrying from every tee.

Strategic play is required from every tee, making the course play considerably longer than its 6,350 yards. The greens have some of the most challenging natural undulations you will ever play and contribute to the wonderful test of golf at West Hill. However, if you are not having your best day, just look around you, breathe deeply and enjoy the wonderful surroundings.

dy Taylor

BURNHAM & BERROW GOLF CLUB
St. Christopher's Way, Burnham-on-Sea, Somerset, TA8 2PE
Telephone: +44 (0) 1278 785760
Website: www.burnhamandberrowgolfclub.co.uk
Architect: Herbert Fowler, Hugh Alison, Harold Hilton, Dr Alister MacKenzie, Harry Co
Architect: Handicap certificate required – contact in advance

Average Reviewers' Scor

Reviewers' Comments

Burnham is a fantastic links course which must be played... Perhaps the most underrate course in England... It has all the elements of classic golf – true greens, a great set of short holes, blind shots and plenty of dunes... Greens were unbelievable – quick, true and tricky and all this in spring... On the 420-yard par 4 8th I hit driver, driver, 5 iron to the green, then four putted as my 20ft downhill putt ran off the green giving me a 60ft return. As I walked onto the 9th tee I was a broken man! Greens in early March were simply superb, as good as the very best greens in summer... Front nine is tougher and better than the back... There are a few great holes in the opening nine with a couple les so at the turn but overall the quality shows through... There are several holes, which an club would love to claim... Holes in the dunes are amazing... Friendly clubhouse... This course made our trip really special.

ırnham & Berrow Golf Club was founded in 1890 and soon after, they hired a ›ungster called J. H. Taylor. His task was to be the club's first professional and ›eper of the greens. One of the great triumvirate, Taylor went on to win the pen Championship five times.

s a traditional out-and-back links course, framed by sandhills and it's a ıallenging layout, too, with tumbling fairways laid out in narrow valleys, otected by deep pot-bunkers and thick rough. The greens are fairly small, quiring precision approach shots and once you are on the putting surface, the n really begins. Burnham's undulating and slick greens are amongst the very best Britain.

ıere are many notable and varied holes and a strong collection of par threes. ıe first six holes are especially good and the back nine is magnificent. Burnham ›ses with a classic 18th, one of the best finishing holes in golf, a dogleg left over ınes and an intimidating long second ot across another ridge of dunes wards a green protected by deep ›reatening pot-bunkers.

ıe club has played host to many ›portant amateur championships ›er the years and the course is gularly used for Open Championship ıalification. It's an absolute must for ıks purists.

The following passage was published in Henry Cotton's Guide to Golf In The British Isles and was written by Fred Bradbeer who was then the club professional: "This is a testing seaside course as a range of sandhills runs along the right hand side of the back nine, with rough grass on the other sides. Leave the fairways, which are on the narrow side, and you are in trouble. I find it difficult to single out any hole as the toughest, for the wind always seems to be blowing across the course."

WOBURN GOLF & COUNTRY CLUB
Little Brickhill, Milton Keynes, Bucks, MK17 9LJ
Telephone: +44 (0) 1908 370756
Website: www.golf.discoverwoburn.co.uk
Architect: Charles Lawrie
Visitors: Contact in advance – midweek only

Average Reviewers' Score

Reviewers' Comments

Beautiful setting and a very severe test of golf... Shorter than the Duke's, but still retains the beautiful pine surroundings that really are such a great feature... I defy anyone not to fall in love with this place... I can still remember every hole... It doesn't have the big tricky greens like its brother the Duke's but it more than makes up for it with its charm... Greens are small and well protected... If your short game is good, you'll score here... Makes you think that little bit more... Tight narrow fairways the order of the day... Leave your driver in the car; you can get into serious trouble... If you are not straight off the tee here you will be penalised every time... Scoring well on the Duchess is a real test... One of the most picturesque courses in the country... You will want to play it again and again and again... Best lunch I have ever had at a golf club... Woburn provides a superb golfing experience.

ıe Duchess is the shortest and prettiest of the three courses at Woburn Golf ub. Major competitions, accolades and honours are usually heaped on the ıkes, and more recently, the Marquess urses. Nevertheless, the Duchess is lightful in its own right, and a serious allenge.

ıarles Lawrie designed the course and opened for play in 1979. It measures espectable 6,651 yards from the back es and it's a fine undulating woodland urse, carved through pine trees. It's hter and less forgiving of the wayward ot than the Duke's so you will require e full repertoire of shots to find the ıall greens in regulation.

ıis is definitely a course where you ust keep your ball in play. If you anage to do this from the tee, then the wards can be great. Use your driver aringly because this is a real thinker's urse. The towering pine trees make ch hole appear exceptionally tight. owever, on occasions, you will need to for distance.

ıe Duchess fits into the Woburn family ceptionally well.

Alistair Tait writes:
The Duchess Course is sometimes considered to be the least challenging of the three Woburn courses, the junior sibling lying in the shadow of well respected and much heralded family members. However, like many younger siblings, it's not a charge the Duchess takes lying down. Nor is it one recognised by true aficionados. Anyone who has played the course knows this is a layout that demands as much respect as the adjacent Duke's and Marquess courses.

The Duchess may not measure the same length as the Duke's and Marquess, but it has pride of place in the Woburn set-up. Rather than act as the "third course," it's a layout that fully complements the other two. The Duchess has its own unique features, its own history. And lest anyone be in any doubt as to its place in the Woburn ethos, here's a telling sign: whenever the members fancy a few holes on their own on a quiet summer's evening, usually it's the Duchess they turn to.

ADDINGTON GOLF CLUB
Shirley Church Road, Addington, Croydon, Surrey, CR0 5AB
Telephone: +44 (0) 208 777 1055
Website: www.addingtongolf.com
Architect: J. F. Abercromby
Visitors: Welcome – contact in advance

Average Reviewers' Sco

Reviewers' Comments

It's an absolute dream… With ravines and valleys, it's hard to believe that you are in the middle of town… Difficult to think of a better course inside the M25… A tad short for today's game but very nice to play… Course really gets going from the 7th a tricky sho Par 3… 9th is a 90-degree dogleg where you have to cross two ravines via two wooden bridges… 12th is a stunning downhill hole and the 13th might just be the greatest Par 3 in England and certainly Surrey… On the 14th tee you have a fantastic view towards th City and Canary Wharf on a clear day… You feel sheltered from the world once inside the gates… Old, traditional and totally absorbing, this is a real hidden gem… I would happily play here every weekend for the rest of my life - it is that good… It's hard to believe that golfing heaven is in Croydon… Play it and prepare to be blown away.

you've never visited the Addington Golf Club and Mr Spock beamed you onto ıe first tee, you would never believe you were a mere ten miles from the centre f London. It's an extraordinary heathland golfing paradise, which has remained ırtually unchanged since J. F. Abercromby – the man behind Worplesdon designed it back in 1914 and many believe it's Abercromby's finest creation. "He ad admirable material, the country of sand and heather and birch trees, and with hat an artistic eye he used it!" wrote Darwin in his book, Golf Between Two Vars.

the early days, the Addington boasted two golf courses, the Old and the New. nfortunately, the New course no longer exists – a housing estate now stands its place. The current course is an idiosyncratic affair, with rickety trestle ridges spanning glorious heathland dells. Mature pine and birch trees provide wonderful feeling of intimacy. It really is a delightful place to be, especially in ıe winter, because the sandy course drains perfectly and remains bone dry nderfoot.

he course measures slightly more ıan 6,300 yards and opens up with a hallenging par three. The 5th hole is a ›ng par four with a slight dogleg to the ːft. An accurate tee shot is required to ıe right to the left-sloping fairway. A anging lie is often the order of the day ›r the second shot, which is uphill to a ell-guarded green. Take plenty of club ›r the approach shot, which is usually ›nger than it looks.

The following passage was published in Henry Cotton's Guide to Golf In The British Isles and was written by Bill Mitchell who was then the club professional:
"Addington offers the golfer every type of golf shot. The dogleg and semi-dogleg holes are a feature of the course, as are the hanging lies for the second shots, where skilful putting is required on the tricky sloping greens. At the 9th, 10th, 13th and 17th holes, the tee shots are played over ravines, trestle bridges rewarding the accurate golfer."

m Spurge

Trevose (Championship)

TREVOSE GOLF & COUNTRY CLUB
Constantine Bay, Padstow, Cornwall, PL28 8JB, England
Telephone: +44 (0) 1841 520208
Website: www.trevose-gc.co.uk
Architect: Harry Colt, Sir Guy Campbell
Visitors: Welcome – contact in advance

Average Reviewers' Score

Reviewers' Comments

Trevose benefits from a wonderful location on the North Cornwall coast… On arrival you are greeted with the most fantastic panorama of the course and rugged coastline beyond… As good as it gets and will soon be the top Cornish links course… Recently lengthened and in immaculate condition with fast, true and undulating greens. It will shortly host more championship events… Wonderful condition with fast and true greens… Excellent test and was in tremendous condition, especially the greens… Start and end of the course certainly are the most interesting… Highlight is the range and mix of par 3s which all offer real satisfaction for a shot well played to the heart of the green. Influenced heavily by the strength and direction of the wind, it is a constantly changing challenge… After finishing with a strong par 4, it is very welcoming to then retire to the clubhouse for a meal and enjoy the views across the bay… Everyone should enjoy this course… A golfing heaven.

·evose is an exhilarating windswept links where little else other than dune ·asses survives in the bleakness and also it's a stern test of golf, especially when e wind is up.

he crumpled fairways are generous in width and the rough is kept short to keep the speed of play and prevent too many lost balls. Some regard Trevose as bliday golf, but the course is technically challenging and will test the very best blfers.

irdie opportunities are there for the taking on the three short par fives, but ake the most of it because many of the ır fours are aggressive and supremely ıallenging. Five of them stretch out ver 400 yards. The short holes are also emorable and exciting, especially the ·d, measuring 166 yards and the 199-ırd 11th, with its two-tiered plateau ·een.

Gary Lenaghan – Professional writes:
Trevose is a most beautiful layout which sits in the mouth of Constantine Bay. On almost every hole you can enjoy the magnificent view out to the Atlantic Ocean and the imposing headland.

The course plays differently every day, dependent on the severity and direction of the always-present wind. The fairways provide generous targets but should they be missed, the rough and bunkers can prove treacherous. Hitting the greens in regulation is never enough to secure par as they slope subtly with some big rises from front to back. Once finished, retire to what must be one of the finest views from any clubhouse.

Walton Heath (New)

WALTON HEATH GOLF CLUB

Average Reviewers' Score

Deans Lane, Walton on the Hill, Surrey, KT20 7TP, England
Telephone: +44 (0) 1737 812380
Website: www.whgc.co.uk
Architect: Herbert Fowler
Visitors: Contact in advance - weekends limited

Reviewers' Comments

The name is a bit of a misnomer as in truth it's only a handful of years younger than the Old... The surroundings are amazing with heathland everywhere and a beautifully crafted course, intertwined with the Old... The New breaks you in gently and then it gets tough... Simply stunning and great fun... Some superb holes set in amongst stunnin card-wrecking heather... Stay straight and scoring isn't too difficult but the heather lines fairways and hides balls amazingly well... Par 4 1st is driveable, as is the 4th and combine with easy par 3 2nd makes it an easy start... Not far behind the Old... Much better tha its current ranking... A perfect day is playing both courses, and in this day and age very good value for money! Superb golf club with great food and staff... I reckon that Walton Heath could make the best composite 18 holes of heathland golf on the entire planet... Quintessentially English.

Walton Heath Golf Club

ıe New course at Walton Heath Golf Club was designed by Herbert Fowler d opened for play in 1907 as a nine-hole layout. Fowler extended it to 18 holes 1913.

ɔth courses – Old and New – are intertwined and have a very similar look ıd feel. The Old is tougher, although e New is a demanding course with emorable holes of great variety. Taking e two courses together can only be ɛscribed as a real treat.

fter a gentle start (the first two holes ɛing pleasant, but straightforward), e New course really starts to show ; mettle. The heather comes into play ıd the holes progressively become ore challenging. There are six par fours easuring over 400 yards in length; the roke index 1 is a massive 469 yards ɔm the white tees.

would be remiss not to mention James aid when writing about Walton Heath. aid loved the Heath and he was the ub professional from 1904 to 1950. ɔr much of his life, he lived at Walton ı the Hill, close to his beloved golf ɔurses. He proudly called his house ırlsferry after his birthplace in the ingdom of Fife.

Ken Macpherson – Professional writes:
Together with the Old course, the New has always been chosen by the U.S.G.A. as the 36-hole venue for the U.S. Open Championship Qualifying, which is quite an accolade.

Colourful heather surrounds the fairways and is also to be found on the faces of many of the bunkers. Whereas the Old course has the most testing of starts, the New requires low scoring on the early holes because after the sixth hole there is only one more short hole – the 200-yard tenth – to come.

Both courses can be fearsome tests should the wind be blowing and the Championship tees be in use. For the more modest player, forward tees, wide fairways and a fast running course will be a more enjoyable and memorable experience as long as the wind is not blowing!

Royal North Devon

ROYAL NORTH DEVON GOLF CLUB
Golf Links Road, Westward Ho! Devon, EX39 1HD
Telephone: +44 (0) 1237 477598
Website: www.royalnorthdevongolfclub.co.uk
Architect: Old Tom Morris and Herbert Fowler
Visitors: Telephone in advance

Average Reviewers' Score

Reviewers' Comments

Westward Ho! is golf in all its simplicity and beauty – a time-warp to the past... Loved every second! Wonderful feeling to this course... Links golf at its most natural... Can't imagine how they keep it in such great nick with all those sheep and horses... Towards the middle of the round, I began to appreciate the subtleties... You need to know where you are going and I would have liked a caddy... Fairways are common land, so horses and sheep are possible hazards... Fowler's greens complexes are brilliant... Got into all sorts of trouble and lost balls galore... 5th and 6th have to be experienced to understand the wonderful imagination of Fowler... 9th may be one of the great short par fives in existence...Watch out for the sea rushes... Interesting course that is challenging and entertaining... Nothing manicured but definitely worth playing... Fabulous venue, lots of history and a joy to play if you like links golf "au natural".

Richard Hughes

oyal North Devon, or should we say Westward Ho! This fabulously nostalgic ıd monumental links course fits firmly into the "must-play" category. In 1864, /estward Ho! opened for golf and it remains the oldest course in England ill playing along its original fairways. It is also the oldest links course outside cotland and home to the second oldest ladies' golf club in the world, founded in 868.

To go to Westward Ho! is not to make a mere visit of pleasure as to an ordinary ourse;" wrote Darwin in his book, The Golf Courses of the British Isles. "It is, s is the case of a few other great links, a reverent pilgrimage. Was it not here ıat Mr Horace Hutchinson and J.H. Taylor, besides a host of other fine players, arned the game?"

Vhen you look out of the clubhouse cross the course, you might struggle to efine the holes. They simply blend into ıe surroundings. There are no trees or edges, except if you count the brambles ongside some of the fairways. There re, however, plenty of reeds and rushes aiting to catch the wayward shot. ossibly, the only sound you will hear is ıat of the wind and if you are lucky, the ound of galloping hooves. Here at Royal lorth Devon, the sheep and horses ave life membership. Don't forget the cal rule – if your ball ends up in a hoof ıark, you may drop without penalty.

Mike Wilson - Professional
Royal North Devon Golf Club is England's oldest golf course, established in 1864. The course was laid down by god, improved by Old Tom Morris and later retouched in 1908 by Herbert Fowler. It's a true links, with sheep and horses still helping to keep the fairway grass short. The course is a great test of golf, with a real likeness to St Andrews, challenging to all golfers and a traditionalist's dream, with deep sleepered bunkers, hard, fast undulating greens and course design that requires every shot in the bag. The clubhouse is also a museum dedicated to the history of golf, and the club's favourite son, five times Open winner J.H. Taylor.

chard Hughes

LINDRICK GOLF CLUB
Lindrick Common, Worksop, Notts, S81 8BH
Telephone: +44 (0) 1909 475282
Website: www.lindrickgolfclub.co.uk
Architect: Tom Dunn, Fred Hawtree
Visitors: Contact in advance – not Tue and weekends

Average Reviewers' Score

Reviewers' Comments

Just about the friendliest welcome in golf… Great course with excellent crisp turf. Testing for the very best players… Categorising Lindrick is quite difficult, it's not really heathland, nor is it moorland, but whatever it is, it's great golf… A picture in the spring when the gorse is in bloom… Superb condition with well-drained fairways and firm, fast greens, even in winter… Best holes are across the busy road… Some of the truest and fastest greens I've ever played on in England... Bring your best putting game… Bunkering is a delight and the course provides a true challenge for the handicap golfer… With so much history and tradition, Lindrick is a must-play course… A genuinely delightful place to play golf… Bring your jacket and tie along if you want to drink or eat in the main bar… Fantastic historic clubhouse with the Ryder Cup room for those not wanting to wear a jacket and tie… Try it alongside Notts for a fantastic twosome.

ıdrick Golf Club is remembered passionately because it was here in 1957 that ·eat Britain and Ireland beat the USA to win the Ryder Cup. Victory had been ong time coming; the last time GB&I had defeated the dominant Americans ıs way back in 1933 at Southport & Ainsdale. After the 1957 Lindrick triumph, e Ryder Cup remained firmly in the grasp of the USA until 1985 when, at the ılfry, a combined team of GB&I and Europe managed to wrestle the cup from e Americans.

ıdrick is laid out on prime common land and the excellent turf has a mixed athland and moorland feel. It's a wild but picturesque course with silver birch-ed fairways, heather and gorse. The fairways are generous and immaculately nditioned, the greens are subtly borrowed, lightning fast and well protected bunkers. Accuracy, rather than length, is critical at Lindrick. We are stating e obvious here, but it is much more ısirable to play from manicured ırways than dense rough.

ıere are a number of strong holes and e 4th, a short par five of 478 yards, certainly fun and memorable, with a ıwnhill drive and a blind approach to ıidden green, nestling in a hollow. The ßth is a 210-yard par three. It's unusual end with a par three and cruel to ıve such an exacting final tee shot, pecially if the match is finely poised.

The following passage was published in Henry Cotton's Guide to Golf In The British Isles and was written by John Jacobs who was then the club professional:
"When I came to Lindrick in 1924, as an assistant professional, the course was open common land, but since then oaks and silver birches have been planted… The 472-yard 4th hole causes the most trouble as you are playing a blind second into the green. Bernard Darwin, our great golf scribe, said this hole was the worst on the course, but he added that it must never, on any account, be altered."

Royal Ashdown Forest (Old)

ROYAL ASHDOWN FOREST GOLF CLUB
Chapel Lane, Forest Row, East Sussex, RH18 5LR, England
Telephone: +44 (0) 1342 822018
Website: www.royalashdown.co.uk
Architect: Archdeacon Scott
Visitors: Restrictions Tue and weekends – contact in advance

Average Reviewers' Score

Reviewers' Comments

Terrific course in a beautiful setting… It's not a course for novice golfers… Some of the carries are fairly daunting and there is thick, ball-eating heather waiting if you miss the fairways… Not too long but plenty of variety and some carries to concentrate the mind off the tee… Some subtle changes have been made to the course in recent years… New tees have been constructed on the 7th and 13th… 5th has been reshaped… Some trees and furze bushes have recently been removed, which has vastly improved the course… Course is playing better than ever… Greens were excellent, smooth and bobble-free but never easy… Always in good condition, although it can get quite hard and bouncy in summer… If you want a fun, not overly long, tricky, challenging golf course then this is for you… Will definitely return, not least because of the friendly attitude of all the staff, from the Secretary's Office to the Pro Shop and bar staff… A fantastic round of golf.

Kevin Murray

'innie the Pooh and Christopher Robin had many adventures here in the dark d mysterious Ashdown Forest. Winnie invented "Poohsticks" here, a game e reckon is even more popular than golf! Oh, and by the way, watch out for uncing Tigger.

ne Ashdown Forest is protected by Acts of Parliament – no alterations are owed to the terrain without the conservators' approval. It is doubtful that e course would have remained so naturally beautiful without having these strictions in place.

ne 6th, the "Island Hole", is one of the best short holes anywhere. It's only 125 rds long from the medal tees, but it's aught with danger, surrounded by a eep stream and a gully. If you hit the een, well done, but two-putting is not sy. There is a ridge running right across e middle of the green.

ne setting is stunning, affording fantastic ews from the high parts of the course ross the forest and the rolling Sussex untryside. The resident professionals bviously like it here too. In Royal shdown Forest's long history there ve been only three pros and Martyn ndsborough, the current pro, has erved a mere 17 years at the club!

Martyn Landsborough – Head Professional writes:
If you go down to the woods today at Royal Ashdown Forest Golf Club the only surprise you will get is that after over 100 years of play very little has changed. The fact that the course has no sand bunkers at first seems to detract from the difficulty of the course but nothing could be further from the truth. The sloping fairways, well-protected greens and the heather infested rough immediately respect your attention.

Each hole is different, each memorable, each with its own challenge and each surrounded by the quiet magnificence of Ashdown Forest.

gel Carpenter - Royal Ashdown Forest Golf Club

SAUNTON GOLF CLUB
Braunton, North Devon, EX33 1LG
Telephone: +44 (0) 1271 812436
Website: www.sauntongolf.co.uk
Architect: Frank Pennink
Visitors: Book in advance – handicap certificate required

Average Reviewers' Scor

Reviewers' Comments

One of the friendliest clubs in the southwest and the guys in the pro shop looked afte us really well... Perfect place for a full day of golf... Wild and rugged sand dune setting make this an inspirational place to play golf... Fast greens, some blind shots, and is a gr little links course in its own right... From an interest perspective, the West has an edge over the East... "Pulpit", the par three 16th is a cracking hole but honestly there are n weak holes on the course... It's not of championship length, but it has everything going for it and it's an exacting test of golf... Need to be on top of your course management and have your wits about you, especially off the tee... Plenty of nuances here... With two courses of this quality, Saunton should be at the top of any serious golfer's must-p list... It's fabulous and a must for links lovers... West is definitely the real deal... It's a little cracker!

Rod Wiltshire

n the edge of Bideford Bay and the estuary of the River Taw, lie the ountainous Braunton Burrows – one of the largest systems of sand dunes England. You'll find Saunton Golf Club amongst these dunes, adjacent to the eautiful and unspoilt North Devon oast.

he West is the second course at unton and it's shorter than its older ster – the East – but, nonetheless, the Vest represents a fine test, measuring ,403 yards from the medal tees. Host a number of County Championships nd the EGU Seniors Championship, it hallenges the very best golfers and is a orthy understudy to the East.

oth courses at Saunton have par set : 71, but the configuration of holes on ne West's inward nine is unusual. Three ack-to-back par fours in the middle nd three par threes and three par fives terspersed at the beginning, and then gain, at the end. A number of narrow reams come into play and many of ne holes feature doglegs. Apart from ne opening hole, which plays directly rough towering dunes, the rest of the ourse plays over pleasant undulating nks land, where the dunes are far less nposing.

Albert MacKenzie - Club Professional writes:
Saunton West is the perfect sidekick for its wonderful partner, the East. Club selection from the tee is paramount as positioning the ball is the key to successfully negotiating your way round the West.

The two opening holes, dogleg in nature, set the tone for what is to follow and too much club from the tee can prove disastrous. The West is graced with five par 3s, all different in distance and direction, and a variety of clubs will be required to find the targets. The "loop" on the back nine, comprising the 12th, 13th and 14th, is arguably the best stretch of golfing terrain offered by Saunton, and it will prove to be as testing in nature as it is pleasing to the eye.

Having co-hosted many national Championships alongside the East, the West is truly a Championship course on its own merits.

ISLE OF PURBECK GOLF CLUB
Corfe Road, Studland, Swanage, Dorset, BH19 3AB
Telephone: +44 (0) 1929 450354
Website: www.purbeckgolf.co.uk
Architect: Harry Colt
Visitors: Telephone in advance

Average Reviewers' Score

Reviewers' Comments

A testing course in a stunning location… Breathtaking scenery, played with a stiff wester wind. Very, very testing round of golf… Ideally, play this course on a windy day to fully appreciate the difficulty of a superb course by the sea… This heathland course is very traditional, a great joy to play and a pleasure to be in such surroundings especially when the gorse and heather are in full flower… There are some spectacular holes… The 5th i exceptionally scenic, the 6th is an attractive and demanding par 5 and the par 3 11th is a particularly daunting hole… If playing in the evening, watch out for the big deer with eve bigger antlers! Stunning views from the high parts of the course… Looking forward to playing again soon as I really enjoyed it and views really are amazing… A lovely place to play golf… Very enjoyable… A must for any golfer… Would I go back? Most definitely!

Andy Taylor

e vista from the Isle of Purbeck golf course is breathtaking, for the course is sitioned on a high heathland plateau and the 360-degree panorama continually errupts one's concentration of the game at hand. To the south across the lent is the Isle of Wight, to the east across Poole Bay is Bournemouth, to the rth across Poole harbour is Brownsea Island and Poole Harbour, beyond and ng to the west, the Purbeck Hills. If there is a golf course where you could drag ur non-golfing partner along, this is it. He or she will be more than happy to ink in the views.

hile this is seaside golf, this is not links golf; Isle of Purbeck Golf Club is set in ieathland nature reserve, decorated with a profusion of gorse, heather, rare ra and fauna. The club was founded way back in 1892 and was modified at the rn of the 20th century by one of the all-time great architects, Harry Colt. Enid yton and her husband once owned the Isle of Purbeck Golf Club and no doubt e surroundings inspired her writings.

urnemouth is not necessarily regarded as the most popular location for a rious golfing break, but there are some fantastic courses to be played, including st Dorset, Broadstone, Ferndown and Parkstone. We think, though, that the Isle Purbeck is the best golf course in Dorset. The view from the elevated 5th tee worthy of the green fee by itself; it's one of the most scenic tee shots in the iole of Britain.

Wiltshire

Ferndown (Old)

FERNDOWN GOLF CLUB
119 Golf Links Road, Ferndown, Dorset, BH22 8BU
Telephone: +44 (0) 1202 874602
Website: www.ferndown-golf-club.co.uk
Architect: Harold Hilton
Visitors: Contact in advance – not Thu and restricted at weekends

Average Reviewers' Score

Reviewers' Comments

Ferndown is an easy walking and challenging golf course set amongst pine trees, heather and rhododendrons... Lovely old course set in a beautiful part of the country and it compares well with some of the best of Surrey's heathland courses... Course management critical... Great use made of the gentle terrain with plenty of bunkers that are very playable and consistent... Beautifully presented course wandering in and out of trees... Winds its way through the pines and its condition was outstanding in all respects... Greens of every shape and size putting to a very good speed, so two putts never guaranteed... Set-up is excellent, as is the turf... A splendid experience... I was impressed with the warm and friendly welcome, they really make you feel at home... First class and a really friendly club too... Well worth a visit for all those who like classic heathland courses... Excellent course, recommended... A great day out... Perfect.

Rod Wiltshire

ːrndown Golf Club is a pine and heathery heaven, set in pleasing manicured ɔuntryside and located a mile or two north of the popular seaside town of ɔurnemouth. This is where Peter Allis learnt his trade, for his father, Percy, was ıe professional here for more than a quarter of a century.

ıe club was founded in 1912 and Harold Hilton, one of the finest amateur ɔlfers of all time, designed the course. It opened for play in 1914. Hilton won the ·itish Open championship as an amateur twice, a feat only surpassed by Bobby ·nes, who was British Open champion on three occasions, also as an amateur.

ıe Old course at Ferndown Golf Club plays across a sandy outcrop of land ·here there is a proliferation of heather and pines. It's an inherently pretty golf ɔurse and sometimes Ferndown is bracketed alongside Augusta because of its ımaculate tee to green grooming. The hazards at Ferndown are subtle – there e the obvious heather and trees to avoid, but the bunkers are especially well ːsigned and positioned. The steep-lipped sand traps are invariably visible from ıe tees and the fairways and they certainly concentrate the mind. Many of the ɔles are dog-legged in shape and tee shot position is critical, rather than sheer ·ngth. Ferndown is a course where scoring well depends entirely on whether or ɔt the ball is kept in play.

Peter Alliss writes:
Ferndown is where I learnt my golf from my father, Percy who was professional at the club. I therefore learnt my early golf in the Bournemouth area, which was blessed with a number of delightful courses consisting of heather, gorse, silver birch and pine.

ndown Golf Club

ST MELLION GOLF & COUNTRY CLUB
Saltash, Cornwall, PL12 6SD
Telephone: +44 (0) 1579 351351
Website: www.st-mellion.co.uk
Architect: Jack Nicklaus
Visitors: Telephone in advance

Average Reviewers' Score

Reviewers' Comments

Possibly the best course I've ever played... Some of the holes are absolute genius, whether it meant 150-yard carries over lakes to find a fairway, to greens that appeared about 10 feet wide... I've never played a better or more demanding course... Some very pretty holes... Mounds on some holes look anything but natural... It's very penal at time even for a slightly wayward shot... Back nine was a bit of a slog... Fact that you had to hit the ball very straight or you could be in trouble just added to the enjoyment... Foun every hazard on the way... I'll definitely come back to try again... I won't hurry back ... Buggy is an absolute must... Entertaining and fun, a great adventure, no easy holes and difficult to score well... Some excellent holes and some I'll remember for as long as I pla golf... The local pro said that Jack must have had a sense of humour when he designed this one!

Rod Wiltshire

will come as no surprise to
ɔte that the Nicklaus course at
Mellion is the course that Jack
ıilt. This is the place to come if
ɔu really want to test your game.
ıe course opened for play in
988 and has already hosted the
ɜnson & Hedges International
pen for six years from 1990 until
995 with Olazábal, Langer and
ıllesteros amongst the winners.

Mellion is located in the
ɜautiful Tamar Valley where
evated tees provide a good
ew of the task in hand. Keep the
ıll in play. There are plenty of
ınkers and loads of water. There
no doubt that this is a great golf
ɔurse and bears the hallmark
f a designer who pays attention
ɔ detail. Many of the greens are
ulti-tiered and the hazards are
rategically placed, making for
timidating tee shots.

David Moon – PGA Golf Operations Manager writes:

"I knew it was going to be good but not this good" a quote from Jack Nicklaus when he played his signature course at St Mellion for the first time. I could not agree with him more when I first walked on to the 1st tee, thinking about some of the greatest players to ever play the game who had stood here in anticipation, just like me. This course does not disappoint. As soon as you walk over the brow of the hill to play your 2nd shot to the 1st hole, you know you are somewhere special and continue through the rolling hills that sculpt the course. The first four holes provide a tough but stunning start to your round and then you get to the 5th tee, a truly wonderful par 4 where you could be anywhere in the world.

This course has the feel of an American-style course with something extra to finish the front 9, a hole that would grace any true links course. Just when you think it cannot get any better you enter the back 9. The run from the 10th to the 13th is probably the closest you will get to Augusta's "Amen Corner", with the 11th and 12th as true stand-out holes and the 18th, which has seen many a close finish. A perfect end to a proper golf course that will keep you coming back again and again.

THE WISLEY
Mill Lane, Ripley, Surrey, GU23 6QU
Telephone: +44 (0) 1438 211022
Website: www.wisleygc.com
Architect: Robert Trent Jones Jnr
Visitors: Members and their guests only

Average Reviewers' Score

Reviewers' Comments

I can remember playing here as though it was yesterday... The conditioning was simply stunning and I have yet to play a course in the UK that matches the Wisley for quality... Most noticeable for me was the absolute definition between the cuts of grass and the rough was penal... I couldn't personally split the three nines, except in character... It's a bit too Americanised for my liking... There's a lot of water, which comes into play often and with a higher than normal degree of difficulty... It's a tough track... My favourite holes are the 3rd on the Garden and the 9th on the Mill... Customer service is so high that you have a feeling of being in another world... The thing that sticks in my mind most was the attentive but understated service... This is a quality venue and if you get the chance to play it, even as a second reserve, jump at it.

Wisley Golf Club

oncealed behind the Royal
orticultural Society's gardens at Wisley
es one of the most delightful private
embers' clubs in the British Isles. There
a strong partnership between the
HS and The Wisley Golf Club and it's
pparent from the moment you arrive at
his prestigious venue. The RHS provides
dvice and guidance to the Golf Club
n shrubs and flowers and, in turn, the
olf Club helps the RHS with turf grass
sues. It's a beautiful partnership.

Vith 27 secluded holes, set out across
ore than 200 acres, the Wisley is a
g golf course. It opened for play in
991, the first course in the UK to be
esigned by Robert Trent Jones Jnr.
he Trent Jones design philosophy is to
reserve the natural beauty of the site
hile creating a playable course rich
ith strategic variety. His objectives have
een fully met here at the Wisley, with
nany holes offering a wide selection
f risk and reward choices, thanks to
xtensive landscaping.

he Wisley is certainly world-class and
you are given the opportunity to play
ere, take it immediately.

Denis Pugh – Director of Golf writes:

The Wisley is a haven for golfers with a passion for the game. It is a stunning mixture of Robert Trent Jones Jnr design and immaculate course presentation. The 27-hole layout allows members and their guests to choose an 18-hole combination from three 9-hole loops named: Church, Mill and Garden.

Although not overly long, at just under 7,000 yards from the championship tees, The Wisley is a stern test. Bounded by the river Wey and the Wey Canal and with seven man-made lakes, water hazards are the centrepiece of the architect's challenge. Cunningly placed mature trees and colourful shrubs add to the visual treat and make additional demands on the player's skill. The beautifully maintained, bent grass greens roll fast and true, even in the most difficult weather conditions.

The signature hole (Mill 9) has severe rough and strategically placed bunkers on the left and water all down the right. Colin Montgomerie is the club's Honorary Vice President and he regards this as one of the toughest holes he has ever seen!

Visley Golf Club

SOUTHPORT & AINSDALE GOLF CLUB
Bradshaws Lane, Ainsdale, Southport, Merseyside, PR8 3LG
Telephone: +44 (0) 1704 578000
Website: www.sandagolfclub.co.uk
Architect: James Braid
Visitors: Welcome except Thu, Sat & Sun am

Average Reviewers' Score

Reviewers' Comments

This is no poor relation to the other 'bigger' names in the area… It's subtle, has clever bunkering locations and it makes you think… It adds to the run of brilliant courses on this stretch of coast… It's certainly not long, but in a way, it's all the better for it… Do not go here expecting huge dunes, as the layout is really quite flat… The greens are excellent… Heather had a tinge of purple and is best avoided, as it is tough to play from… Good golf is rewarded and poor shots are punished… Deep bunkers surround most of the quality greens… Great paced greens with a tough starting hole, but the best hole is the 16th – Gumbley's – which runs alongside the rail track with views across to Hillside GC… Enjoy the spacious clubhouse and have a look at the super photos/ memorabilia of the past Ryder Cups… It was nice to play the course in its centenary year! Well worth playing.

Kevin Murray

)nly the Belfry has hosted more home soil Ryder Cups than Southport & .insdale. But everybody flocks to play S&A's royal neighbour, Birkdale. If only they new what they were missing a couple of miles down the road.

&A has a very natural feel, although it is somewhat old-fashioned with some lind drives and obscured approach shots. This is not your traditional out-and-ack layout. In broad terms, the course is laid out in two loops, the first seven oles forming the inner loop. The fairways wind their way through gaps and alleys between the dunes and many of the greens are raised on tricky-to-hold lateaux. It's a serious golfing test, the layout measures over 6,600 from the back ees with par set at 72 and from the yellow tees, the length drops to 6,250 yards, ut the par also drops down to 70.

here are many memorable holes but none more so than "Gumbley's". The par ve 16th measures 506 yards, playing directly into the prevailing wind and, when ne wind's up, three solid strikes will be equired to reach the green. The hole as a fine example of a sleeper-faced unker. It's a monster, set into the face f a large, tussocky sand ridge. Avoid this ne like the plague.

outhport & Ainsdale should be played ot only from a historic perspective ut because this is a very natural and hallenging links course, one of Braid's nest seaside examples.

James W. Finegan writes:
Possibly taking its cue from its ampersand mate Royal Lytham & St Annes, Southport & Ainsdale opens with a par three, a 180-yard carry over thigh-high rough to a fiercely bunkered (nine deep pots) and fiercely undulating green. This links, laid out by James Braid in 1923, is endearingly old-fashioned with its blind and semi blind shots, low mounding sometimes serving as a welcome backstop at the green, and an occasional cross bunker deceptively short of the putting surface.

vin Murray

LUFFENHAM HEATH GOLF CLUB
Ketton, Stamford, Lincolnshire, PE9 3UU
Telephone: +44 (0) 1780 720205
Website: www.luffenhamheath.co.uk
Architect: Harry Colt, Charles Alison, James Braid & C.K. Cotton
Visitors: Welcome, contact in advance

Average Reviewers' Score

Reviewers' Comments

Luffenham Heath is a pretty course set on high ground… It's a very special golf club… Tees, fairways and greens were all superbly kept and a pleasure to play on… For the time of year the course was in good condition, the tees were firm and well mown and the greens were consistent… Easy to underestimate the difficulty of the course… Pace and deceptive undulations make putting a real challenge… Course was a good if somewhat forgiving test with some very nice holes… 17th is a superb hole as is the 7th, where the green site is a masterpiece… Describing it as a heathland course is unfair to those that are… Character of the course is mixed but its predominant feel is one of heathland rather than parkland, and whilst the sub-soil may be largely clay, years of top dressing have resulted in excellent playing surfaces… Club's heritage and attention to detail is apparent throughout… All in all an enjoyable round… A pleasant place for golf.

ıtland Water is the largest man-made lake in Western Europe, set in the middle ' England's smallest county. Three miles south of Rutland Water, as the crow es, is the Earl of Ancaster's Common ith its peaceful and tranquil golf course. feeling of calm washes over as soon as ɔu drive into the car park.

he course is laid out principally in an ıt-and-back fashion, but the holes are ɔuted in every conceivable direction. /hen the wind blows – as it often ɔes on this undulating and elevated ɔmmon – it hits you from all directions. espite the numerous trees and ıshes which line many of the holes, ɔu never feel hemmed in. Most tee ıots are pleasantly inviting. Measuring 315 yards from the back tees against par of 70, Luffenham is by no means championship challenge but it is an ıtriguing test.

he golf is good and honest and there e some excellent holes. Luffenham eath is a course to enjoy rather than slog round and you will find the golf finitely pleasant and, at times, rather xhilarating.

John Ingleby – Club Secretary writes:

This heathland course is rightly known as a 'little gem'. Blessed with many fine holes the course is a classic test for golfers. The dipping and arcing 2nd has all Luffenham's challenges in one hole as does the 7th with its carry over gorse and fiendishly sloped green. Perhaps the last four earn more plaudits than any other stretch of the course. Two strong par fours and a long par 5 finish sandwich the Heath's signature hole, a devilish par 3, a downhill beauty over a tangle of mounds and studded with wicked bunkers.

The course has recently undergone major renovation and modernisation under the guidance of Dr Martin Hawtree. It has been a tremendous success, turning what was always a pleasant and engaging task into an eye-catching fresh and daring challenge without compromising the natural delights of the soothing landscape, designated as a Site of Special Scientific Interest.

ROYAL WORLINGTON & NEWMARKET GOLF CLUB *Average Reviewers' Score*

Golf Links Road, Worlington, Suffolk, IP28 8SD
Telephone: +44 (0) 1638 712216
Website: www.royalworlington.co.uk
Architect: Tom Dunn, Harry Colt
Visitors: Welcome midweek and after 12.00 Sat and Sun - contact in advance

Reviewers' Comments

A delightful and traditional course... Superb design on such a tiny plot of land... Course has some interesting holes... This course is subtle. It is an inland links of the traditional kind. It ignores the world of manicured fairways and pristine bunkers... It did not in any way meet my expectations... I was left bemused at how it rates as highly as it does... 5th is the best hole by far on the course but the rest, unfortunately, didn't impress... It has not changed since the day it was built some 110 years ago and that is its charm and its strength... It still ranks as one of my favourite places to play... A traditional and genuine honest course... From the quirky little clubhouse to the immensely tough second and the driveable 9th, it is an amazing little gem squeezed into a tiny plot of land... Great nine-holer... If you want to play golf from a hundred years ago and appreciate historical quirkiness rather than grandeur, then I recommend it.

›yal Worlington & Newmarket Golf Club probably has the finest nine-hole golf urse in the world. It was certainly an incredible achievement to fit nine holes ›to such a tiny piece of sandy ground and it's the only nine-hole course ever to ›ve been voted onto a Top 100 list.

; a classical golf course, often referred to as Mildenhall and it's the home of ·lf for undergraduates at Cambridge University. The turf has all the qualities of ;easide links, free draining and springy. Make sure you bring your best putting ›me – the greens are lightning-fast and tricky to read.

·m Dunn, who laid out the course in the early 1890s, reputedly said: "God eant this land to be a golf course". Some 30 years later, Harry Colt lengthened and little has since changed. Jo Floyd holds the course record. In September 49, he went round nine holes in incredible 28 stokes. He holed his cond shot at the opening par five for albatross two; this obviously lifted his irits for the rest of the round!

ıree and four-ball play is not allowed at 'orlington, foursomes and twosomes e the order of the day. Whatever you ›, do not let this traditional approach ›t you off playing this amazing nine- ›le course; it offers the ideal golf day, pecially if you can safely negotiate the famous short 5th hole.

Bernard Darwin writes:
Worlington is not unlike Frilford in appearance, being extremely solitary, flat and sandy, and dotted here and there with fir trees. There are only nine holes, but of these several are really excellent, and none can fairly be said to be dull. One curious feature of the course is that one may play a round there which shall be made up almost entirely of fives and threes. This was conspicuously the case in the days of the gutty ball, for there were four holes that could be reached from the tee, although the second hole certainly required a very long shot, save for colossal drivers.

HINDHEAD GOLF CLUB
Churt Road, Hindhead, Surrey, GU26 6HX
Telephone: +44 (0) 1428 604614
Website: www.the-hindhead-golf-club.co.uk
Architect: Unknown
Visitors: Welcome midweek and after 12.00 Sat and Sun - contact in advance

Average Reviewers' Scor

Reviewers' Comments

Recognition at last for one of Surrey's finest... In terms of unsung heathland courses, th is up there... It's the significant elevation changes which make Hindhead so endearing... The front nine is spectacular... Some superb holes, particularly on the front nine where you hit along valleys to elevated greens, it then begins to tail off before coming on stron for the last few holes... With no poor holes and just a handful of average ones, this is a great course in its own right, distinctive and not just a cheap imitation, and both classy and traditional whilst not snobbish or exclusive... Condition is awesome, especially the famous quick greens... Greens are some of the fastest surfaces you can find... The members call the walk from 5th green to the 6th tee cardiac hill... Was in awe of the beauty of the surroundings... It is one of those non-championship must-plays... A place that you can truly call home.

ndhead Golf Club was founded in 1904 and it was the inspiration of a number golfing enthusiasts. It is therefore "elementary, my dear Watson" that Sir ·thur Conan Doyle was among the original founders.

ıe Devil's Punchbowl is a large hollow of dry sandy heath to the west of ndhead and it's overlooked by Gibbet Hill, which is the second highest hill in ırrey. The front nine at Hindhead is laid out through these heather-strewn Ice ;e valleys and the back nine plays on the hillside heathland plateau. The location not only breathtaking it's truly beautiful.

ıe front nine is one of the most dramatic and memorable outward halves in ılf, but the back nine also represents fine golf on ideal golfing terrain. The 3rd one of the best par threes in Surrey and the par three 6th, the signature hole at requires a mere flick with a wedge, is also rather special. The holes continue enthral and just when you think you've cracked it, you're faced with the timidating tee shot at 17, where the right-to-left sloping fairway is extremely ugh to hold.

James W. Finegan writes:
The course can fairly be said to have a schizophrenic personality, or at the very least, a split between "top" and "bottom". The 1st hole and the entire second nine are routed over the high ground, a gently rolling plateau some 800 feet above sea level. Conversely, holes 2-9 are played down in a valley, through a couple of long gullies and over ground with abrupt ups and downs.

vin Murray

LITTLE ASTON GOLF CLUB
Roman Road, Streetly, Sutton Coldfield, West Midlands, B74 3AN
Telephone: +44 (0) 121 353 2942
Website: www.littleastongolf.co.uk
Architect: Harry Vardon, Harry Colt
Visitors: Contact in advance – not on Saturdays

Average Reviewers' Score

Reviewers' Comments

Little Aston is set in a salubrious area where the rich and famous Brummies live... It's quiet and peaceful despite being so close to Birmingham... It's immaculate, especially in the summer and this tree-lined course is an oasis.... Mature trees flank most of the hole and the bunkers are well positioned and well maintained.... Bunkering is quite superb... good honest parkland course in immaculate condition... Holes are varied and offer up a excellent challenge... Little Aston has been hyped up as one of the best parkland course in the land... I enjoyed it but somehow I expected a little bit more... Don't forget your jacket and tie or you'll be in the side bar – this is a traditional member's club. Well worth playing if you like parkland courses.

:tle Aston Golf Club is set in 176 acres of tranquil, mature parkland in the rmer grounds of Little Aston Hall. The club is hidden away on the edge of :clusive suburbia, eight miles north of Birmingham city centre.

arry Vardon reputedly laid out the course in 1908 for ten guineas. He had a arming and elegant piece of parkland to work with and succeeded in creating obably the best and toughest true parkland course in England. As it turned out, rdon had created a course with long and challenging carries that ultimately oved too hard for the members, so Harry Colt was summoned to make the urse friendlier. Mark Lewis (the club's professional for over 40 years during e first half of the 20th century) must also be credited for taking Little Aston rough to maturity.

ne course is always maintained maculately and even in the winter, it ays well for a parkland layout. They are stifiably proud of the quality of their 'ge greens and of their trademark rdon cross-bunkers. The undulating rmal tree-lined fairways ensure that u get a private and picturesque walk the park.

Patric Dickinson writes:
The greens of Little Aston are large, beautifully kept, and exceedingly cunning. They are such greens as Professor Einstein would delight to putt on – for there is no such thing as a straight line however, superficially, it may appear so. The slightest of inclines, the subtlest, finest of borrows and curling declivities bear the ball away to touch the hole like a tangential arc.

As you stand upon the clubhouse terrace you face westward, and look beyond the park to a rising countryside of pasture; it is impossible to believe you are only a few miles from the vast industrial sprawl of Birmingham.

WEST LANCASHIRE GOLF CLUB
Hall Road West, Blundellsands, Liverpool, L23 8SZ
Telephone: +44 (0) 151 924 1076
Website: www.westlancashiregolf.co.uk
Architect: Ken Cotton, Fred Hawtree
Visitors: Weekdays only, not before 9.30am

Average Reviewers' Scor

Reviewers' Comments

A belter! There are two circles of nine holes with the front nine, in particular, having a somewhat natural, wild feel to them... The beauty of this course is its variety... The key to the course is keep the ball on the fairway... Hugely underrated... This is a cracking links course... It doesn't favour either hook or cut, it's just important to hit the fairway. Six par fours over 400 yards suggests a very long course but the four par threes are of average length, so a fine balance of length and difficulty is maintained... The prevailing wind was directly in our faces over the last four holes which made for a difficult finish.. Probably the ugliest clubhouse I have ever seen, but who cares when the golf is as good and challenging as this... Tough test when the wind blows up on the last 4 holes...A grea course... Tough little cookie... A real test!

Jim McCann

'est Lancashire is the oldest surviving golf club in Lancashire, founded in 1873. 1901, Harold Hilton, one of the finest amateur golfers of all time, was the cretary of West Lancashire Golf Club. That same year, he won the British nateur Championship at St Andrews, beating J Low by one hole. Hilton was so the British Open champion in 1892 and 1897, a feat only surpassed by obby Jones, who won the British Open on three occasions, also as an amateur. aturally, the club is proud of its association with Harold Hilton.

ne course was originally designed by the hands of an unknown architect, but is is such a natural links that we suspect Nature did most of the work. We know that Ken Cotton and Fred awtree made significant revisions to e layout in the early 1960s.

s esteemed Royal neighbours keep 'est Lancs out of the limelight but it is truly classical links course, located on charming stretch of prime links land. n a clear day, to the north, Blackpool ower can be seen in the distance. To e southwest, there are panoramic ews across the Crosby Channel to the rkenhead peninsula and Liverpool Bay eyond.

Stewart King – Club Secretary/ Manager writes:
Only in Britain can one sample the true flavour of seaside golf, of which West Lancashire is a perfect example. Within the framework of the coastal dunes and the railway, a glorious balance unfurls. There are humps and hollows, greens on plateaux and greens in dells, contrast and comparative shelter in the inland holes and everywhere a sea of rough sandy wilderness to punish the wrongdoer. On summer evenings, as the sun casts its shadows on the links, the shipping slips quietly by on the Irish Sea and there is time to reflect the distant beauty, the realisation occurs that the West Lancashire enjoys the best of all worlds.

PARKSTONE GOLF CLUB
49a Links Road, Poole, Dorset, BH14 9QS
Telephone: +44 (0) 1202 707138
Website: www.parkstonegolfclub.co.uk
Architect: Willie Park Junior, James Braid
Visitors: Contact in advance - handicap certificate required

Average Reviewers' Scor

Reviewers' Comments

What a superb course… It's certainly heathland but it feels very different to the main Surrey courses. This has something to do with the rolling and undulating fairways that have a very links-type feel… Not the longest course even off the back tees but still a thinking player's test… We played off the white tees and it was still short at circa 6,250 yards and, as a pretty short hitter, I was still playing a lot of short irons… A lovely variety of holes with the 3rd, 4th, 10th, 11th and 17th standing out in my opinion… An intimidating 200-yard par 3 finish where anything to the left will kick further left onto the first fairway… Course is set amongst some of the most expensive real estate in the world but there was no stuffiness at all from anyone… Nice to experience the warm welcome from the members, pro staff and clubhouse staff… I look forward to our club's return visit… A must-play example of a tight heathland links style course.

Rod Wiltshire

'e've classified Parkstone Golf Club as a seaside heathland course. It's certainly ›t a traditional links and neither is it very far inland. It's an unusual and unique ›urse, located on a beautiful sandy tract of undulating heathland, affording ›gnificent views across Poole Bay and Poole Harbour. The fairways are lined with e delights of pine and heather and the picture in spring is an especially pretty ›e when the rhododendrons are in full bloom.

›e land was originally part of Lord Wimborne's "Cliffs of Canford" Estate that ›etched all the way out to Sandbanks, a natural peninsula, jutting into the sea the entrance to Poole Harbour. The land was sold to the Water Company and ey built two reservoirs and a pump ›use. Little did they know the water ›uld come in handy to irrigate the new ›lf course that Willie Park Junior laid ›t in 1909. The great revisionist, James ›aid, appeared on the scene in 1937 and rkstone was lengthened and altered ›cordingly. Little has changed since aid's alterations.

›is is 'Alliss' country. Peter Alliss ›rned his trade down the road at rndown where his dad, Percy, was the ›ofessional for 25 years. Peter became e professional at Parkstone in 1957 d remained at the club until 1970. ›cording to The Guinness Book of Golf ›cts and Feats, Percy and Peter are the ›ly family on either side to have father d son representation in the Ryder Cup.

The following passage was published in Henry Cotton's Guide to Golf In The British Isles and was written by Peter Alliss who was then the club professional:
We cannot house big events which draw crowds, because we lack tent space, sufficient car parking area and practice facilities. But we have a very keen membership of 800 players, always ready to bring the best golfers to Parkstone for exhibition matches.

I think our 11th hole from the back tee, 520 yards uphill, is our toughest. The carry is 180 yards to the fairway; heather, trees and gorse line the fairway on both sides and there is a 20-ft drop on the right of the green into real jungle country.

LIPHOOK GOLF CLUB
Wheatsheaf Enclosure, Liphook, Hampshire, GU30 7EH
Telephone: +44 (0) 1428 723785
Website: www.liphookgolfclub.com
Architect: Arthur Croome
Visitors: Contact in advance – not Tue or competition days

Average Reviewers' Scor

Reviewers' Comments

Quaint and picturesque with the ability to suddenly jump up and bite when you least expect it… A pretty and exceptionally challenging heathland track… Deceptive start with a par three and it gets better and better… Shorter par fours make you position the tee shot instead of 'slashing' at it with the driver – strategy is the winner on these holes… For the high handicap golfer it is a good and fair test with every club in the bag required… 13th is a belter… You'll need to keep out of that heather… Greens are excellent, some of the best and fastest I've ever putted on… Sneak onto the back tee of the par four 4th – the hole is fantastic and the view worth a look… In these days of the 7,400-yard championship course, it is nice to re-visit Liphook and play golf in a love setting… Underrated course and it's up there with the best in this neck of the woods. Very friendly members and a hospitable clubhouse.

Rachelle BAxter

ɔhook is as pretty as a picture. A delightful, classic heathland course spanning ampshire and Sussex's county boundaries. It's a course for the connoisseur, not r the dilettante. The club was founded in 1922. A teacher called Arthur Croome iginally designed the course, his one and only.

today's standards, Liphook is relatively short, but with a lowly par of 69, playing handicap is another matter. The heather, pine and birch place a premium on e rather than length. The sandy ground is wonderfully undulating with natural pressions and elevations and, in some ways, the land is reminiscent of that nearby Hindhead, where there is other charming and understated golf urse.

nusually, Liphook opens with a par ree and the bunkers are audacious, aracterised at the 5th, 6th and 11th. ne prettiest holes and probably the st sequence is the trio from the 12th the 14th. If we had to pick a favourite ɔle, we would plump for the 14th, a ort par four doglegging to the right here a bold drive will leave a short tch to the green, and a good birdie pportunity will be on offer following a ell-positioned drive.

phook is classy and does everything ell, but in an understated way. charming course with friendly embers – the perfect venue for golf.

Ian Mowbray – Head Professional writes:

Liphook is a rare gem and is often overshadowed by some of its more illustrious heathland neighbours. The course was the only design of Arthur Croome and was constructed in 1922. Tom Simpson later carried out subtle improvements to the design.

The clubhouse sits high on a hill and overlooks the opening and closing holes, both of which offer a differing challenge. Accuracy from the tee is crucial as the course is not the longest and has relatively few bunkers, but stray into the heather or pine trees, which line most fairways, and you'll struggle to save par. The greens are as good as any you will putt on and patience and imagination are required to make a score.

chelle Baxter

Fulford

FULFORD GOLF CLUB
Heslington Lane, York, YO10 5DY
Telephone: +44 (0) 1904 413579
Website: www.fulfordgolfclub.co.uk
Architect: Major Charles Mackenzie
Visitors: Welcome - contact in advance

Average Reviewers' Score

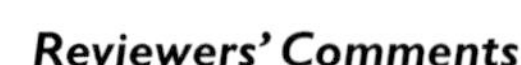

Reviewers' Comments

One of the best in Yorkshire... What a gem of a course – it has not lost any of the difficulty and challenge that it had when it hosted the Benson and Hedges... It's not a championship test these days but it certainly provides some fun for mere mortal handicappers... Despite the mature trees, it's fairly open and inviting off the tee... Was i excellent condition with long punishing rough alongside generous fairways... Can see wl the greens were voted best on European Tour... A stiff test with the highlight being the par 5s, which are varied... Good bunkering and that rough meant you had to earn your score... Very enjoyable, traditional course with an excellent 19th overlooking the last green... Fun, but not all I'd hoped for... Is an easy walk in the park as there are few ups and downs... Was annoyed when I last played here as I forgot to look out for Langer's tree... I strongly recommend this course to anyone... Look forward to returning.

st one mile from historic York lies the magnificent Fulford Golf Club, a club eeped in history, which celebrated its centenary in 2006. After getting the umbs-up from no less than James Braid, the current layout was designed by ajor Charles MacKenzie, brother and business partner of Dr Alister MacKenzie f Augusta fame) and has played host over the years to many important amateur d professional tournaments.

any major winners such as Seve Ballesteros, Nick Faldo, Sandy Lyle and Ian oosnam have graced the fairways of Fulford, when for 20 years the club hosted e Benson & Hedges, Sun Alliance, and Murphy's Cup tournaments, as well as osting the first British Ladies' Open Championship.

ut it is surely the image of a flaxen-haired Bernard Langer, clambering 20 feet the magnificent ash tree by the 17th een to play his third shot from the anches, that sticks in the memory.

s reputation for some of the best eens on the European Tour attracted e likes of Greg Norman, Gary Player, e Trevino and legends like Sam Snead d Billy Casper. The greens were clearly Ian Woosnam's liking in 1985 – he itzed around Fulford in just 62 strokes, ill the 'all-comers' record.

uilt predominantly on sandy heathland, lford features superb turf and provides true test of championship golf.

Guy Wills – PGA Professional writes:
Fulford provides a stern test for golfers of all abilities; the course presentation is of the highest standard, ensuring that golfers enjoy the Fulford Experience. The flat true greens provide excellent putting surfaces and it is easy to see why they were voted best on the European Tour. The course provides a mixture of heathland and parkland golf. Most fairways are tree-lined, so precision off of the tee is key to a good score. Visitors will receive a warm welcome from all at Fulford Golf Club.

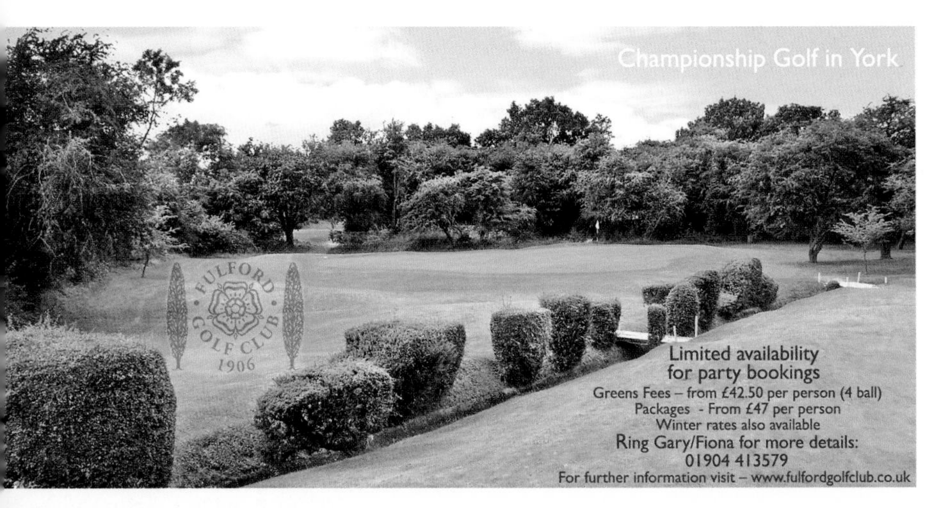

Brocket Hall (Palmerston)

BROCKET HALL GOLF CLUB
Welwyn Garden City, Herts, AL8 7XG
Telephone: +44 (0) 1707 335241
Website: www.brocket-hall.co.uk
Architect: Donald Steel
Visitors: Member's guests only – some packages available

Average Reviewers' Score

Reviewers' Comments

Palmerston course is good, very good in fact... One of the best new courses that I have played... In many ways it's reminiscent of the Marquess course at Woburn... Holes lined by majestic pine trees, mature beech, hornbeam and sweet chestnuts, and others with commanding views from the high points over rolling Hertfordshire countryside and woods... Tough approach shots into the greens made all the more difficult due to the undulations in the fairways... Undulating fairways of Augusta proportions... Use a buggy with the satellite yardages for the full experience... There are many 'wow' holes on the course that will stay in your mind for years... Each hole is very individual and varied - uphill, downhill, dogleg right, dogleg left and only two holes on level ground... Two of the best holes are par 5s: 6 and 13... 6 is a cracker, tree-lined doglegging left to a raised green... A stylish place that comes highly recommended... Playing golf at Brocket Hall is a treat of the highest order.

ɔcated a mere 20 miles to the north of the capital and close to leafy Welwyn arden City in Hertfordshire, lies Brocket Hall. With two courses named after rime Ministers who used to reside at Brocket Hall, the Palmerston is the new d on the block, opening for play in 2000.

he course winds its way through the undulating estate where majestic specimen ees pose as impressive hazards. Donald eel's design philosophy was to provide top quality course with the least ɔssible intrusion on the site. We think e has exceeded his objective.

nlike the older Melbourne course, the iver Lea doesn't come into play on ne Palmerston course. Instead, there's old bunkering to contend with and, f course, avenues of trees. Steel has eated a thinking men and women's ɔurse where the golfer is presented ith options.

Vithout doubt, Brocket Hall is a classy nd stylish place. Add in the famous uberge du Lac restaurant and the tate-of the-art Faldo Golf Institute and ɔu've got a serious golfing venue.

Keith Wood – Professional writes:
The Palmerston is our latest addition at Brocket Hall and is a gem. Cutting through the established woodland of the Brocket Estate, the highly acclaimed architect Donald Steel has been sympathetic to the historic landscape in his design.

His layout continually asks questions of the player's course management, shot-making and general accuracy. The 7,100-yard course has many elevations with strategically placed bunkers providing the tests. The theme continues with the rolling contours of the large greens, making approach play accuracy a premium. The Palmerston is an exciting and fair test for every standard and can be played from a number of tee positions. It provides a wonderful contrast to the design of Brocket Hall's Melbourne course.

London Club (Heritage)

THE LONDON GOLF CLUB
Stansted Lane, Ash (Near Sevenoaks), Kent, TN15 7EN
Telephone: +44 (0) 1474 879899
Website: www.londongolf.co.uk
Architect: Jack Nicklaus
Visitors: Members and their guests only

Average Reviewers' Score

Reviewers' Comments

Beautifully carved new course... Ultra-modern style, the top end of the new courses... tough track, which plays two or three shots harder than you think... Generous fairways that were like fringe greens... Large greens in top condition... If you miss putts, it's your fault as these greens are fantastically true... Six holes feature water and the greenside bunkering is worth a mention, with some having seven bunkers as protection... Big bunkers grouped in perfect position to swallow up your ball... Lots of special holes, favourites for me – par3 7th – all carry over the lake and the short par4 13th, again approach to the green over another lake (thanks, Mr. Nicklaus)... Enjoyed my game but expected a bit more... Could quite easily get used to playing this course week in, week out... The London Club experience is to be remembered, on and off the course you are well looked after... Only for members and their guests, which is a shame, but if you get the chance, take it.

ıe London Golf Club is situated in rolling countryside close to Ash Green d the historic Brands Hatch motor racing circuit. The late Sir Denis Thatcher husband of former Prime Minister Margaret – opened the club in September 93. But the official course opening took place in July 1994 and was marked by Charity Challenge Skins Match on the Heritage. Jack Nicklaus – the Heritage urse designer – battled with Seve Ballesteros and Tony Jacklin. Seve's magical ort game eventually helped him to edge Jack out with ten skins to eight. Tony ıs an also-ran.

'ith wide generous fairways, the eritage is a course that tempts you reach for the driver on many tees, ıt the key to good scoring is in your proach play. The huge USGA greens e well protected by enormous egularly-shaped bunkers, which wait catch the wayward shot. Naturally, icklaus has used water as a feature on number of holes and perhaps one of e best examples of a water hazard is ı the par five 5th where a lake edged stonework guards the green. There e two drop zones on the excellent ır three 7th, indicating that the lake is serious problem and the custodian of ındreds of golf balls. The best water ɔle of all comes at the short par four 3th, which requires an iron off the tee ıd then a short iron approach across e lake to a narrow green. It's a cracker.

Alasdair Robertson – Director of Golf writes:

The Heritage golf course is a true gem, carved out of the Kent countryside and designed by arguably the greatest player the world has ever seen, Jack Nicklaus.

Nicklaus's design style is written all over the Heritage course and can be easily identified by the peppering of cavernous bunkers that adorn every fairway and proudly guard every green. A big emphasis is placed on the golfer regarding driving distance and accuracy, especially when playing from the blue championship tees, from where the course stretches to an impressive 7,208 yards.

The short game plays a major part in building a score around The Heritage course as all greens are large and fast, built to exacting USGA specifications.

WOKING GOLF CLUB
Pond Road, Hook Heath, Woking, Surrey, GU22 0JZ
Telephone: +44 (0) 1483 760053
Website: www.wokinggolfclub.co.uk
Architect: Tom Dunn
Visitors: Contact 7 days in advance – no weekend visitors

Average Reviewers' Scor

Reviewers' Comments

Quality is the key word and the club is currently working hard around the course to maintain the high standard... Having played the 3 Ws of Woking, West Hill and Worplesdon I can honestly say it would be a pleasure to be a member at any. Woking is the shortest and probably the easiest of the three, yet there is enough to keep you interested all the way round... During a hot summer, it's almost links-like... It's good advice to leave the driver at home... Greens with some significant undulations are kep in superb condition... Some heavy tree clearance underway, presumably to encourage the return of heather... One of the easier Top 100 courses I have played... Oh and tho lady members – bless them – I'm sure they are not all the same! Had a lovely day here.. Well worth a visit and in the winter it's a bargain... Classy and traditional... Great cour that looks a treat... Had a lovely day here... Thoroughly enjoyable.

Stuart Abramson

'oking is a charming Old England heathland course, laid out by Tom Dunn 1893. The club was intended to provide relief for a few golf mad barristers ho were sick and tired of playing on muddy clay. We must thank Woking holeheartedly because nobody thought that heather and gorse-strewn land was able ground for golf and this was the first experimental heathland layout.

nere is absolutely no doubt that Woking is located in an idyllic spot and the nusual pavilion clubhouse only adds to the charisma. This is not a championship yout by any stretch of the imagination; e course only measures 6,340 yards om the medal tees. But Woking is a ature and strategic layout requiring ell-positioned tee shots that must, at costs, remain out of the heather and play. We recommend that you leave our driver in the boot of the car to oid any temptation.

'oking is not riddled with bunkers but ose there are, are adroitly positioned. 1900, a controversy raged when two ınkers were dug into the 4th fairway. ne members were mortified that they ight be penalised after hitting a good raight drive. Looking back at this, 'oking was a pioneer in architectural rms, forcing the player to make a ecision, lay up short or bravely aim on e right line.

Bernard Darwin:
Among the heathery courses, we must give a prominent place to Woking, which is the oldest and still one of the best of them. Indeed, although my judgement may not be strictly an impartial one, I think it is still the most entertaining upon which to play, and the golf is undeniably interesting. It does lack something, however, of the bigness of Sunningdale or Walton Heath, which have been laid out on an altogether grander scale.

The keenest golfer among my acquaintances said to me one day that, whatever anybody might say, Sandwich and Woking were the two pleasantest places for a game of golf, and though there is no resemblance between the two courses, I think his verdict was a sound one.

art Abramson

East Sussex National (West)

EAST SUSSEX NATIONAL GOLF RESORT & SPA
Little Horsted, Uckfield, East Sussex, TN22 5ES
Telephone: +44 (0) 1825 880088
Website: www.eastsussexnational.co.uk
Architect: Bob Cupp
Visitors: Contact in advance

Average Reviewers' Score

Reviewers' Comments

East Sussex National is an impressive complex with a very large modern clubhouse and pro shop... It has the US-style welcome with bag drops, etc... An excellent golf course in immaculate condition with some tremendous holes, but like the other course here, it is very long... The West course is a good one, although as with any new courses there are a few fields you play on, but overall, it is a really good test of golf with some cracking holes... Some choice holes, especially the par 5s, which are probably my favourite collection of par 5s of any course I have ever played... Better than the East – the holes are certainly more memorable... It was in great condition, fast true greens, punishing but playable rough... 16th is the weakest hole... 18th is a great hole... I cannot recommend this club highly enough, from the top-notch Americanised service to the top food... It really is good... Worth the visit and we will definitely play it again.

Kevin Murray

ıe West course is the more intimate, and the prettier of the two courses at the st Sussex National Golf Resort. Once the reserve of the members, the West ı now be played as part of a visitor's package.

ıb Cupp designed both courses and they opened for play in 1990. Cupp ed bent grass from tee to green, and the result is an American-styled course, th plenty of definition between the various cuts of grass. The West is the ıger of the two courses, measuring a massive 7,154 yards from the back es. Host to the Challenge Tour Championships between 1995-1998, the West urse represents a serious test of golf. It was also used for the European ur Qualifying School between 1994-1997. But don't be put off: there are four parate teeing areas and the course measures only 6,069 yards from the regular en's tees (5,199 yards from the ladies' tees).

tractive views of the South Downs are part of the package. The ground is dulating and there are plenty of mature trees to negotiate. There are also many emorable holes.

st Sussex National is a stylish golf mplex and there is no doubt that this one of the country's most welcoming d customer-focused golf clubs. A day ying the West and the East will be hausting, but well worth the effort.

James W. Finegan writes:
The West course is less open in aspect and feel than its sister. The surrounding woods are denser and the elevation changes are sharper. There are genuine hills here, and the climbs result in entrancing views over the South Downs... I should mention that, in the best upscale American tradition, the sprawling brick clubhouse has panelled locker rooms and marble-clad showers; the huge pro shop is a veritable temple of merchandising.

ʼn Murray

THE LONDON GOLF CLUB
Stansted Lane, Ash (Near Sevenoaks), Kent, TN15 7EN
Telephone: +44 (0) 1474 879899
Website: www.londongolf.co.uk
Architect: Ron Kirby (Nicklaus Design)
Visitors: Contact in advance

Average Reviewers' Scor

Reviewers' Comments

I have now played both this course and The Heritage and I must say the members here are very lucky to have two wonderful courses at their disposal – The International a very good second best... The International flows better (than the Heritage) and was in fabulous condition on each occasion I have played here... Unimaginative... You can put me down as a fan of the International which I think is every bit as good as the Heritage. I cannot understand why this course is anywhere near the Top 100... I've played both courses and have enjoyed both – for me in the "better than most" category... This is a cracking layout which tests the best golfers... The corner around the 12th and 13th is fabulous with the water your main enemy... Take plenty of balls... I really enjoyed it... Very enjoyable... Wonderful clubhouse and top service make The London Club one of the better contemporary clubs around the London area.

e International course at the London Club is a high-class accompaniment to e Jack Nicklaus-designed Heritage course. The International is the layout that u can play here at the London Club and it's well worth making the effort.

esigned by Ron Kirby under the cklaus Design banner, the International ened for play in 1993 and it represents ough links-like challenge. The gently lling Kent countryside provides fficient elevation changes to make ngs interesting and from the tips, ich measure 7,005 yards, it's a really ugh challenge for all except the very st golfers.

valley separates the outward nine from e inward half, giving the International distinctly different feel and also some ectacular views. Four lakes make atery graves for numerous golf balls d they come into play on five holes. ere are also plenty of sand traps in rious shapes and sizes, from small pot nkers to enormous expanses of sand.

Alasdair Robertson – Director of Golf writes:
If one could compare The Heritage course conditions to the manicured perfection of a South Carolina resort course, then you will doubtlessly draw many similarities to a windblown Scottish links when referring to The International golf course. One could be forgiven at certain stages of the round for believing you were striding the links of Machrihanish or Muirfield, with its rolling fairways and deceiving winds.

The biggest challenge that the golfer faces on The International is any one of its five par three holes, which are dramatic to say the least and protected by some of the largest water hazards you will see on a golf course in the British Isles.

The Heritage may be the more exclusive of the two courses, but for a true golfing challenge, The International is by no means a poor relation. Just different!

BUCKINGHAMSHIRE GOLF CLUB *Average Reviewers' Score*
Denham Court Drive, Denham, Buckinghamshire, UB9 5BG
Telephone: +44 (0) 1895 835777
Website: www.buckinghamshire-golfclub.co.uk
Architect: John Jacobs
Visitors: Contact in advance

Reviewers' Comments
Classy but understated, tremendous and underrated... This club has great attention to detail. The driveway, clubhouse etc were all excellently maintained and this was not forgotten when we reached the course... Far and away the best winter golf course in this region... Very pleasing on the eye, with its shaped fairways and clearly defined cuts of rough... As a young course it shows its youthfulness, somehow you know that this course is but a baby. I firmly believe this course will grow into a classic... Par 3s present no real danger and the three finishing holes lack drama... The run of holes from 6-9 are breathtaking in both beauty and golfing design... Old Jacobs did well... It is not particularly challenging, and not very memorable... This is a stiff test and will suit lower handicap golfers more so than higher... You can score well if you are patient and careful especially at the 7th, 8th, 10th and 12th... Recommended for all good golfers to experience... Worth a visit.

tuated close to the charming and historic town of Denham, the
ıckinghamshire is a big golf course, designed by a big golfer – former Ryder Cup
aptain, John Jacobs.

his elegant course opened for play in 1992 and it's set in more than 200 acres of
ature parkland. They planted thousands of indigenous trees during the building
f the course and they encourage wild flowers to grow in the rough, including
eadowsweet and primula – it's certainly a pretty place.

cobs has created a very natural looking golf course that harmonises with
s surroundings. Additionally, it is an
citing, surprising and challenging
yout. But at the same time, golfers of all
oilities will enjoy it. There are numerous
rge teeing areas to choose from
ıd the huge greens are exceptionally
ceptive, fast and true – among the
est in the area. Plenty of water instils
ıcertainty, waiting to swallow the
ayward shot.

hn Jacobs said: "I believe we have
eated a golf course which contains
terest and beauty for golfers of all
vels, providing either a challenge or a
entle walk round". We agree with big
hn – the Buckinghamshire is delightful.

Paul Schunter – Head Professional writes:
Buckinghamshire Golf Club is a magnificent parkland course and offers a delightful oasis of calm and privacy, bounded and crossed by the Rivers Colne and Misbourne. Our superb John Jacobs-designed course is able to offer a challenge to every standard of golfer, which has been borne out by our hosting of major events sanctioned by the PGA European Tour.

Once you have experienced the challenge of our course, you will be able to enhance the experience by enjoying the elegant surroundings of the historic Grade II listed Denham Court Mansion that forms our clubhouse.

WENTWORTH CLUB
Virginia Water, Surrey, GU25 4LS
Telephone: +44 (0) 1344 842201
Website: www.wentworthclub.com
Architect: John Jacobs, Bernard Gallacher and Gary Player
Visitors: Handicap certificate required – contact in advance

Average Reviewers' Score

Reviewers' Comments
Challengers to the claim that Wentworth has the best set of 54 holes in Britain would be Gleneagles, Woburn and The Belfry. It has to be Wentworth for me and the Edinburgh course is brilliant… From the regular tees, it's challenging and it's not in any way inferior to the elderly East and West courses… It does not look much like its older brother (The West) and older sister (The East) in the sense that this has a modern feel with a pine tree-lined look… So many plus points; short par 4s, long par 4s, doglegs in both directions and one of the best is the 11th – a cracking par 4… Par 3s are not too shabby either, especially the 2nd and 17th… After playing the Edinburgh my pre-round expectations were exceeded. Cannot wait to return; only problem is which course to play, as they are all quality… Many members prefer the Edinburgh… Special place Wentworth… Wentworth has bags of style.

'entworth needs no introduction; after all, the West course is the most
levised course in Britain. Even those disinterested in the game of golf have
ard of the stylish and famous Wentworth Club. But do you really know how
od the Edinburgh course is?

ne Edinburgh is not a relief course, it's 100 per cent the real thing. The East
d West courses are tough acts to follow, and when Wentworth identified 150
res of land between the existing two
urses and Sunningdale, the heat was
n to create something really special.

500 tons of wood was cleared in
cord time by a team of New Zealand
mberjacks and, in 1990, after a huge
fort, the South course opened for
ay. The course was later renamed the
linburgh, in honour of the Duke, who
nducted the opening ceremony.

nis is a driver's course and, with a
rdage that stretches out beyond
000 yards from the back tees, you
n't afford to leave your big stick in the
r. There are so many excellent holes
at it is almost unwise to single one
it, but the long par five 7th is a truly
agnificent three shotter. Many good
ndicap golfers will struggle to reach
is green in three shots.

John Jacobs writes:
I firmly believe, therefore, that a golf course must be capable of testing the very best players and also be able to give immense pleasure to the handicap golfer. Consequently, the Edinburgh course has generous forward tees, and greens large enough to make possible both difficult and easy pin positions.

For the most part, the course winds its way through "The Great Wood", which does call for straight hitting. However, the fairways are not so narrow as to inhibit the use of the driver, rather to encourage it.

The overall balance of the course with its four 5s, four 3s and ten 4s, is orthodox, and yet no two holes are alike. The par 3s are not long (the writer hates long par 3s), but differ greatly in character, the second bearing a striking resemblance to the 12th at Augusta.

STOKE PARK CLUB
Park Road, Stoke Poges, Buckinghamshire, SL2 4PG
Telephone: +44 (0) 1753 717171
Website: www.stokeparkclub.com
Architect: Harry Colt
Visitors: Contact in advance

Average Reviewers' Scor

Reviewers' Comments

A cracking place to play golf… History is evident from the drive through the estate to the old mansion… The 27 holes available provide a combination of challenges… Plenty of variation and a delight to play… Lots of different feels to your experience… Althoug there are plenty of huge trees, you have to be pretty wayward to find them, except perhaps on the 17th... 7th is quite rightly the signature hole and it's fantastic, one of my favourite inland par threes… Greens are huge, true and subtly borrowed… Course left me with an overriding sense that it could not be bothered to try harder to be better than it is… High quality parkland golf course played in a special place… Can easily sit firmly in any list of top British courses and to play here is a treat… One of the best corporate/society venues in and around London… Clubhouse is a fabulous building and the experience is top drawer… A certain taste for the finer side of life here!

:oke Park is located at Stoke Poges, a charming leafy town situated on the fringe f the Chiltern Hundreds. A Hundred is a traditional name for the division of an nglish county and the wooded Chiltern Hills (which separate Buckinghamshire om Berkshire) were once a notorious iding place where robbers would wait ambush. These days, things are more enteel.

:apability Brown originally landscaped ne historic parkland in the late 18th entury. Stoke Park is surely one of the nest parkland golf courses in the South f England. The main line of defence the abundance of huge stately trees nd Colt's clever design. The fairways ppear wide and generous from the tees. owever, it is important to get the line nd distance right, otherwise you will ce challenging second shots.

lore famous than the majestic parkland olf course is the 18th century mansion esigned by James Wyatt (architect to eorge III), housing the clubhouse, hotel nd restaurant. Recently, the course as been extended to 27 holes. Each of ne three loops of nine is named: Colt, lison and Jackson. The original course is nade up of the Colt and Alison nines.

Stuart Collier – Director of Golf writes:

Stoke Park Club, formerly known as 'Stoke Poges', provides everything you would wish from a parkland course. Harry Colt laid it out in 1908 and the genius of his design still offers a great challenge which will take you through every club in the bag.

The front nine is a great test of golf with both par fives offering good birdie opportunities. Tough par fours will test out your approach play and the par three 7th is a gem. Placing your ball on the green will not guarantee a par, as this green is treacherous during the summer months.

Follow in James Bond's footsteps as you complete the back nine playing the 17th and 18th holes. This was the scene for Bond's epic golf match versus Auric Goldfinger. For the third nine holes, accuracy and control are a must. The 21st hole is a signature par three for this nine, played over water and the 'Repton Bridge'.

PRINCE'S GOLF CLUB *Average Reviewers' Score*

Sandwich Bay, Sandwich, Kent, CT13 9QB
Telephone: +44 (0) 1304 611118
Website: www.princesgolfclub.co.uk
Architect: Charles Hutchings, Percy Lucas, Sir Guy Campbell, John Morrison
Visitors: Welcome midweek – contact in advance

Reviewers' Comments

Greens, greens, greens, I think anybody would be pushed to find better greens anywhere... Beautiful links course which was deserted when we played... The greens ar first class – the best I have played on – and the fairways are immaculate... If only all club put this amount of effort in! Sublime true greens and a nice easy walk... A great 27 hole of golf awaits all handicappers... This is another good course to play alongside Royal St George's and Royal Cinque Ports... Not the greatest links course, but there are some great holes... If there are only 18 in you, favour the Dunes, then the Shore... Make sure you play when there is a gale, what fun! The rough is not unfairly long... With this much history in the bank, it deserves a better clubhouse... We were made most welcome an will be returning before too long... What a pleasure to play and a great welcome at the clubhouse... Don't miss the Sunday roast... Play this course if you can!

Kevin Murray

t the turn of the 19th century, it as decided that a new links should e built at Sandwich. The new club ould welcome ladies, juniors and men. harles Hutchings and Percy Lucas laid ut the course on land donated by the arl of Guildford. The 18-hole course, retching out to almost 7,000 yards, pened for play in 1907.

he military commandeered the course uring both World Wars but it was rtually obliterated during the Second Vorld War. Sir Guy Campbell and John orrison were commissioned to re-uild Prince's and were able to save 17 f the original greens and incorporate em into the new 27-hole layout. They ave created a classic "links and a half", ith raised greens, rippled fairways, eep bunkers and, naturally, that famous nks rough.

he Dunes and Shore loops make the "championship" course. The imalayas is shorter but nonetheless, n enjoyable nine holes. Above all, a arm welcome awaits everyone, much it did it when Prince's first opened, 00 years ago.

Robert McGuirk – Head Professional writes:
Set on the edge of Sandwich Bay, Prince's is an outstanding links course with three loops of nine, called The Himalayas, The Shore and The Dunes. The course has fast greens, in excellent condition all year round and there is a premium on accurate driving, with the championship course measuring over 7,200 yards. There are no blind shots, ensuring an extremely fair challenge for visitors.

Prince's has held many prestigious tournaments over the years, the most famous of which was the 1932 Open Championship, which was won by Gene Sarazen. Famously, this was the first tournament in which a sand wedge was used and Sarazen put the club upside down in his bag just in case it was illegal. However, this proved not to be an issue. In past years, Prince's has held major tournaments including The PGA, Open Final Qualifying, PGA Club Professional Championships, The Amateur Championship (co-hosted with St George's), The Ladies' Open and The Curtis Cup. We have many famous members, including grand slammer Gary Player, Phil Mickelson and Sir Michael and Lady Bonallack.

vin Murray

SEATON CAREW GOLF CLUB

Average Reviewers' Scor

Tees Road, Seaton Carew, Hartlepool, TS25 1DE
Telephone: +44 (0) 1429 296496
Website: www.sportnetwork.net/main/s235.php
Architect: Dr Alister MacKenzie, Frank Pennink
Visitors: Welcome after 10am

Reviewers' Comments

Seaton Carew, hidden within industrial Teesside, is proof that a classic course can be found in an apparently unpromising area... A links course for the purist and a fair and honest test of golf... Though not long by modern standards, the wind, dunes, and whins make the course a severe test... TOUGH, TOUGH, TOUGH, I love links golf but my playing partner and I got absolutely destroyed... There are no unforeseen tricks and everything is laid out in front of you except for one semi-blind drive and the odd hidde bunker...You need to hit fairways. If you miss any greens or fairways, your ball is lost and end of story... It's unpretentious and, at the same time, traditional... If you hit a low ba unlike me, and miss the wind, you will love it. Otherwise, bring the A+ game and enjoy t sea air... Friendliest staff on earth will greet you... It is incredible value... The complete experience.

Steve Smith

ere are now 22 holes at Seaton Carew, following Frank Pennink's addition of ur new holes. The members now have a number of playing options. The Old urse, an out and back layout, is the original MacKenzie design. The Brabazon urse incorporates 14 of the original holes; Pennink's four new holes come to play at the turn. The Brabazon, an uneven par 73 (35 out, 38 back), is now nsidered the championship course and is tougher and longer than the Old urse. In 1985, Seaton Carew hosted the Brabazon Trophy (English Amateur roke Play Championship), producing a tie for first place between Peter Baker d Roger Roper.

on't be put off by the industrial surroundings of chimneys and chemical works; is excellent golf course is one of the best on the East coast of England, a real acKenzie treat. There are a few ridges sand dunes and the fairways undulate ntly, but otherwise this is a relatively t links course, always at the mercy of e wind.

e 17th hole, called "Snag", is one of e club's many great holes. The late erek Hornby, a historian and author of e History of Seaton Carew, poetically scribes the 17th. "The seventeenth's ngers are countless, beginning with hin, gorse and dune, the rough and thering bunkers, and the green's dulating tune. To veer even slightly is tal, the cost is distressingly high, many e card that's been torn up, just here ith home, oh so nigh".

Mark Rogers – Club Professional writes:

Seaton Carew is among the ten oldest golf courses in England and boasts a history as rich as its years. It is regularly featured in the golfing press, and justifiably so, as it is a truly wonderful and testing links which has hosted a range of prestigious R&A and EGU Events.

Set within industrial Teesside, but on a Site of Special Scientific Interest for rare orchids among other things, it is always a pleasure to play. As is the case with all great courses, it demands a variety of shots, and the use of every club in the bag.

Seaton Carew Golf Club
Tees Road, Hartlepool TS25 1DE
Telephone: 01429 266249
Fax: 01429 267952
www.seatoncarewgolf.co.uk
seatoncarewgolf@btconnect.com
"The real memorable hole is the 17th, Snag (a definite understatement) an Alister MacKenzie original. A study of it alone justifies a visit to Seaton Carew."
Donald Steel

Hanbury Manor

HANBURY MANOR GOLF & COUNTRY CLUB
Ware, Hertfordshire, SG12 OSD
Telephone: +44 (0) 1920 885000
Website: www.hanbury-manor.com
Architect: Harry Vardon, Jack Nicklaus II
Visitors: Member's guests and residents only

Average Reviewers' Score

Reviewers' Comments

Hanbury Manor is a special place to visit... Great setting and an overall interesting course... Course has improved and matured enormously... The rough is up and the fairways are immaculately defined... It's probably in as good a nick as it ever has been... They have just finished a bunker refurbishment and they looked and played amazingly... Layout is well designed and has excellent, true greens... Uses the contours to provide a variation of shots... The front nine is a bit open but the back nine more than makes up for it... A straightforward, yet nonetheless, charming course in a lovely setting... A track that will suit all handicap levels, yet be challenging enough for the low handicapper... A real pleasure to play... Play it if you can, it is a real gem.

ıe Jacobean-style manor house ıs built in 1890 for the Hanbury nily and in 1923, it was ›nverted into a girls' boarding hool. It remained a school until '86, when it was ambitiously ınsformed into a luxury hotel d the prestigious Hanbury anor Golf & Country Club.

ıe club's tournament potential ıs quickly recognised and, in '96, Trish Johnson won the 'omen's European Open by five ear shots. The following year, the en's PGA European Tour arrived the shape of the English Open ıd the tournament remained at anbury until 1999.

anbury Manor stands on its vn in an area absent of great ılf courses. There's a lovely nbience here, an English rural rsion of an American Country lub.

Daniel Blesovsky – Professional writes:
Harry Vardon originally designed a nine-hole course set amongst the grounds of a majestic Jacobean Manor House in the 1900s. It wasn't until 1990 that Jack Nicklaus II and the Golden Bear Design Company re-invented Hanbury Manor's nine-hole Vardon course to create what I believe to be one of the finest inland golf resorts in the UK.

The front nine overlooks the idyllic Hertfordshire countryside and provides an American links-style opening to the round. The course then meanders around the imposing manor house and through the daunting oak trees to form a beautiful parkland back nine steeped in history, boasting two of the original Harry Vardon-designed bunkers.

We've played host to the Women's European Open and Men's English Open for three consecutive years. The course was said to be a great favourite for the players on the European Tour.

The course appeals to all levels, playing from 5,360 yards off the forward tees to 7,052 yards off the Championship tees. Lakes, bunkers and tight run-offs protect the large USGA greens, where an accurate approach shot will be required to avoid the hazards. Once on the green, you will see a typical Nicklaus design, with slopes and very subtle borrows resulting in a stern test of putting.

Hanbury Manor is an interesting test of golf with double fairways and an abundance of water; no two holes are the same, so it is tough to choose a favourite.

BOVEY CASTLE
North Bovey, Dartmoor National Park, Devon, TQ13 8RE
Telephone: +44 (0) 1647 445016
Website: www.boveycastle.com
Architect: J.F. Abercromby, Donald Steel and Tom Mackenzie
Visitors: Welcome contact in advance

Average Reviewers' Score

Reviewers' Comments

It's come a long way since the re-design... Doubt there is a more pleasant place to play golf anywhere in the world... The moor is an ever-present and inspiring feature and the castle is quite beautiful in an understated way... Front nine is far and away the better of the two halves... Front nine is exceptional and the back nine less so... It would pay dividends to switch the nines around... Course is good fun and I enjoyed myself... Enjoyable... It's not a championship layout but it represents a thoughtful challenge... Holes that skirt the river are tight and memorable... 3rd and 7th are simply great golf holes... Be prepared to lose a few balls the first time round in the river and the woods. The staff make service in the US look ordinary, they do it with style... Whole experience is five star... If you want to stay and play somewhere special in the English west, then Bovey takes some beating.

Bovey Castle

vey Castle is located on the very edge of Dartmoor and the magnificent house is built in 1906 for Lord Hambledon. "The Great Western Railway Company ught it and turned it into an hotel," wrote Bernard Darwin in an article for untry Life which was later reprinted in his 1934 book, Playing the Like, "and en, with Mr Abercromby to show them how, made this most charming of golf urses at its garden gate."

nn F. 'Aber' Abercromby, the master English architect who fashioned the brilliant orplesdon and Addington, laid out the course at the Manor House Hotel and it ened for play in the Roaring Twenties. e hotel enjoyed prosperity for many cades, then, slowly but surely, it fell o disrepair. With vision and drive from itish entrepreneur Peter de Savary and ittle help from Donald Steel and Tom ackenzie, the Bovey Castle course was -born and the new beauty opened for ay in the summer of 2004.

n short," wrote Darwin, "this is the eal course to have at the end of the rden. There never was one better ited to a cheerful foursome, for ere is plenty of scope for strategy in ciding who is to drive against who, and which of the river holes."

Richard Lewis – Golf Professional writes:
John Abercromby, one of the finest architects of his time, designed Bovey Castle in the 1920s.

Individuality is a vital feature in the make-up and charm of any golf course. Indeed, Bovey's unmistakeable individuality is a synonym for uniqueness. This is particularly apparent on the first eight holes, where the Bovey and Bowden rivers come into play on every hole.

The course measures 6,303 yards for a demanding par 70. In these days of 7,000-yard courses, our yardage may seem tame, but there are few courses that are more challenging, memorable or attractive.

vey Castle

Moor Allerton 73

MOOR ALLERTON GOLF CLUB
Coal Road, Wilke, Leeds, Yorkshire, LS17 9NH
Telephone: +44 (0) 113 266 1154
Website: www.magc.co.uk
Architect: Robert Trent Jones
Visitors: Contact in advance

Average Reviewers' Sco

Reviewers' Comments

Stunning! The first 18 (The Lakes) is an absolute joy to play… A thoroughly challenging and enjoyable 27-hole course… A tough test, particularly from the back tees… Whole course has a very grand American feel – sweeping fairways and big, undulating greens… Well worth playing alongside the more traditional Alwoodley and Moortown… Some of the shorter par 4s are something to behold – I especially enjoyed the 3rd teeing to a downhill fairway to attack an elevated green… Par 3s are great also, excellent bunkering and water hazards... Greens were the best I've played on all year… For those who dislik the stuffiness and tradition of many top clubs, Moor Allerton is refreshingly laid back, enjoyable and very hospitable… It's a lot better than many Open Qualifying venues and has some ambience in being the first RT Jones design in the UK… Could not fault the visual appeal of the course… Picturesque views all around… Very enjoyable… A must visit course.

Moor Allerton Golf Club

oor Allerton was originally founded in 1923 and Alister Mackenzie laid out the iginal 18 holes close to Moortown. Later, the club moved a few miles away to e present site because it was "bursting at the seams". None other than the nous Robert Trent Jones designed the new course – his first in the British Isles and it opened for play in 1971.

nes laid out 27 holes on 220 acres undulating Yorkshire countryside, in ree distinct loops of nine holes. Each ne starts and ends at the welcoming Vaterhole" halfway house and you'd wise to replenish your energy levels cope with Jones's design philosophy, here a par is tough and a bogey is the rm.

early Moor Allerton contrasts with near neighbours, Alwoodley and oortown. The Moor Allerton style is odern and American – big contoured eens, large teeing areas, long boldly-aped bunkers and, of course, water zards. Having said this, the layout ends beautifully into the delightful ndscape to combine the best of rkshire and America. It's friendly and laxed off the course, but as tough as ils on course.

Richard Lane – Professional writes: Moor Allerton is a wonderful sanctuary for any golfer. Blessed with a modern 27-hole golf course, designed by eminent architect Robert Trent Jones – his first project in the U.K. The golf course meanders through some of the most scenic undulating countryside in Yorkshire. The flora and fauna complement the many natural water hazards that truly enhance your enjoyment. Deer and Red Kite, although timid, can often be spotted during a round.

Large bunkers, lakes, elevated and undulating fast greens are the charms here. We probably have some of the best, consistently fast greens in the country, which are both challenging and fun to play on. The variety of risk and reward challenging holes can appeal to any level of golfer without detracting from their enjoyment. I could never tire of playing here, due to the golf course possessing such a wide variety of holes.

oor Allerton Golf Club

THE OXFORDSHIRE
Rycote Lane, Thame, Oxfordshire, 0X9 2PU
Telephone: +44 (0) 1844 278300
Website: www.theoxfordshiregolfclub.com
Architect: Rees Jones
Visitors: Contact in advance

Average Reviewers' Scor

Reviewers' Comments

The Oxfordshire demands respect... A modern monster... No expense has been spare in the creation of this beast... Is as artificial a course as you will find anywhere – but it is an awful lot of fun... If you are more of a traditionalist, you may find it a bit contrived That said, it's a great day out... Great course to play with everything strategically placed to catch you out... Could become a very hard slog on a cold, blowy day... Clearly designed for competition golf, it relies heavily on water to provide some unique challenges... Many memorable holes... Par 3 5th and 13th really stand out, as does the sublime and exiting 17th... 8th and the 17th holes are outstanding and require tough choices to be made... Very exciting course... If you want to experience 'stadium' golf, definitely try this one out... Great course for competent golfers who are not afraid of making a cricket score if they have an off day!

ʻou like tradition, then steer clear of The Oxfordshire. If you are seeking citement, this might be the course for you.

ie prolific golf course architect Rees Jones designed the course and it opened r play in 1993 after significant earth works. Jones is big in the States, and has ısigned many courses, including the design of the South course at Torrey nes and Bethpage's Black course, host the 2002 US Open.

stensibly, it's a tournament course with od vantage points for spectators. The &H International Open was held here four consecutive occasions (1996-99). nes, Langer, Clarke and Montgomerie ere the respective winners. In 1996, ura Davies won the Ladies' English pen here too.

ıe 17th is the nerve-wracking signature ɔle, a downhill par 5 with a right to ft dogleg. A huge lake runs all the way ɔwn the left of the fairway. The green opposite the lake. The safe but longer ute is to play around the water, but if u're feeling lucky, you could go for it ross the lake with your second shot.

Stephen Gibson – Head Professional writes:
The Oxfordshire, set in the rolling hills of the Chilterns, is located approximately 45 minutes drive northwest of London on the outskirts of the historical university town of Oxford. It was designed and built by the world-renowned architect Rees Jones, his first course in Britain.

No expense has been spared in creating this beautiful course. A tactical blend of bunkering, strategically placed lakes, wispy rough and wind make this a real challenge. Combine that with its natural beauty and you have the only course you'll ever need. The Oxfordshire also offers one of the finest clubhouses in the country with conference facilities for up to 200 people, a fabulous restaurant that provides Continental and Japanese cuisine, a lounge bar, a spike bar and a traditional Ofuro bathhouse.

BAMBURGH CASTLE GOLF CLUB
The Wynding, Bamburgh, Northumberland, NE69 7DE
Telephone: +44 (0) 1668 214321
Website: www.bamburghcastlegolfclub.org
Architect: George Rochester
Visitors: Welcome - contact in advance

Average Reviewers' Scor

Reviewers' Comments
This is a fun gem... Of all the courses I have played, there are no finer views. Beaches, castles, hills, islands... It's not the longest, but has the most spectacular views, bettered only by Pebble Beach and Kapalua... A hidden gem, and is definately the best course in Northumberland... It's short but it's not easy and for the first time of playing you'll nee to study the yardage chart carefully. Better still, play with somebody who knows the course... There are a number of semi-blind shots, even to the par 3s which are simply amongst the best collection of one-shot holes on any course I've ever played... Can't give this course a high enough rating... Take my advice and make the short detour off the A1 on your way up to the Home of Golf and play Bamburgh Castle... If you get clea weather, this will be the highlight of your golfing trip... I defy you to leave without a big smile on your face, and the intention to return.

Sam Coles

imagine that the golfer's eye must be more often taken off the ball at Bamburgh an on any other course," wrote Bernard Darwin in his 1920s book Golf on e LNER, "the view is so compellingly beautiful that we really have to look at it, matter how critical the shot. First of all of course there is the Castle which gorgeous beyond words, as it stands huge and menacing on the top of its eer wall of rock, looking out to sea. Then in the middle distance are the Farne ands and away to the left across a stretch of water and sandy headlands we e another castle, small by comparison, but looking very splendid, perched on stony pedestal, Holy Island, Lindisfarne. Altogether there may be prettier golf ourses, but I really don't think that I have ever seen them, and I have seen a od many by this time."

iere are many scenically stunning golf ourses around England's long coastline it there are none more glorious than imburgh Castle. Its elevated clifftop te provides a natural platform from hich to drink in the 360-degree views id also the topography provides for me truly memorable holes. According the R&A Golfer's Handbook, George ochester originally fashioned Bamburgh astle. The course opened for play in 904 and was apparently later revised, it the vast majority of this 5,621-ird par 68 layout remains as it was ick in the times of Bernard Darwin those years ago... including the arm welcome in the old pavilion-style ubhouse.

Alan Patterson – Secretary/ Manager writes:
One of Northumberland's finest golf courses awaits you at the beautiful village of Bamburgh. Perched on basalt outcrops overlooking the village and ancient fortress, from which the club takes its name. The course is often regarded as the most picturesque in England and it's a delight to play. There is more to the course than scenery, however, being a fine test of golf for all those who play it, and a regular venue for county and inter-county events. Add a charming clubhouse and you will appreciate that your golfing trip to Northumberland is not complete without a visit to Bamburgh.

ıvid Metcalf

BROADSTONE GOLF CLUB
Wentworth Drive, Broadstone, Dorset, BH18 8DQ
Telephone: +44 (0) 1202 692595
Website: www.broadstonegolfclub.com
Architect: Tom Dunn, Harry Colt
Visitors: Contact in advance - No fourball play

Average Reviewers' Score

Reviewers' Comments

Although not as well known as its Surrey counterparts, this heathland course is as good if not better than many and always in excellent condition... Good layout that uses changes in elevation to very good effect... Great heathland course with many stand-out holes, the best being the 4th, 7th, 13th, 14th and 16th, which are among the very best in the country... Good selection of tough par threes and strategic par fours make for the best golf you will find in Dorset... Pleasant course but nothing special. Par 4 13th the exception which is a great golf hole... Needs to follow the lead of Parkstone and start cutting back the trees to open up the dramatic vistas and restore the heather... Greens are generally small and well defended... The clubhouse serves good bar food and the welcome was warm and sincere... A good venue for a day's golf if in the area.

Rod Wiltshire

roadstone is laid out on glorious rolling terrain. The elevated homeward nine rovides panoramic views of the Purbeck Hills and Poole Harbour. Measuring 315 yards from the back tees and 5,467 yards from the forward tees, roadstone is not a championship layout. Having said this, a number of important nateur tournaments have been held here, testing some of the very best golfers. nd although Broadstone cannot offer length from the tee, it can offer beauty, ith profusion of heather, gorse, birch and pines. In many ways, it's a shorter, ross between Sunningdale and Walton Heath.

roadstone takes slow play seriously nd, consequently, four-ball play is not lowed. Do not let this put you off this is undoubtedly an outstanding eathland course and worthy of clusion on any serious golfing itinerary.

feel entirely at peace with roadstone," wrote Darwin, "which has ome really fine holes, and is as pleasant spot to play golf in – as breezy, and retty, and quiet – as anyone could esire."

Mathew Wilson – Professional writes:
Broadstone Golf Club was originally known as the Dorset Golf Club, when Lord Wimborne founded Broadstone in 1898. Tom Dunn, a prolific designer of his day, was commissioned to design the course. Harry S. Colt was later commissioned to redesign Broadstone, utilising a glorious tract of heathland to the west of the railway line to build seven new holes.

Thus, Broadstone became a quintessential heathland course and little has changed since. Each of the holes has got a very definite character of its own. This allows you to play the course over and over again quite clearly in your mind's eye.

DELAMERE FOREST GOLF CLUB
Station Road, Delamere, Cheshire, CW8 2JE
Telephone: +44 (0) 1606 883800
Website: www.delameregolf.co.uk
Architect: Herbert Fowler
Visitors: Contact in advance

Average Reviewers' Score

Reviewers' Comments

This hidden gem reminds me of Hillside's parkland parts... What a stunning golf course... A throw-back to the old days of golfing... Brilliant course, never thought a course could be this good in the winter... Beautiful in the summer and always in great winter condition... Very hilly and beautiful features... Set in splendid Cheshire countryside, with plenty of breathtaking views to admire, whilst overcoming the tough challenges each hole has to throw at you... The course itself has a wonderful array of holes snaking through lines of ancient trees and frustratingly difficult heathland... Hard Par 3s that take your breath away... Will play again and again, a must for all golfers... Immaculately presented... A course that few know about and for my money that's half its aura... Can't wait to play again... Hidden gem is the correct term for this wonderfully sculptured golf course.

Paul McMillan

Delamere Forest Golf Club is one of the counties hidden gems," writes John Mulder – Club Secretary. "Despite the word 'Forest' in its title, Delamere is a natural heathland course. Certainly, trees are part of the strategy on several holes, but, in general, Delamere Forest provides a glorious backdrop to the panoramic views from the higher parts of the course.

Fowler had no qualms about asking the golfer to undertake a number of blind drives, carrying some considerable distances and enjoying the healthy exercise of hill climbing. Overall, there is much variety in hole lengths and every kind of shot will be called for, but the opening five holes really stretch the average player.

There are many holes with character, for example the 5th, with a long uphill carry to the green, a pond to the left and below the green, and the need to hold the shot up to that side. The 6th is a short hole from an elevated tee to a small green set at an angle to the tee with enticing views over the pond below the green to the left, with woods and fields in all directions. The 8th requires a long straight tee shot to find a narrow fairway to give a long iron shot to a steeply sloping green. This hole was reached from the medal tee in the 1970s by one of our past members, Mr George Johnson. The 15th hole is a dogleg left with a blind drive over a hill and an out of bounds in the forest on the left. The raised plateau green is situated in a delightful dell with a bell to be rung to tell those behind that the coast is clear, with the finishing hole having a rough patch of reeds just short of the green. The course leaves and returns to the clubhouse twice and players cross at the 6th and 16th tees."

Martin W. Brown – Club Professional writes:
Delamere Forest is a glorious sandy heathland course that plays hard and fast in the summer. Play for position from the tee to get the best angle of approach to the greens to avoid dropped shots. The holes vary in distance so you can expect to use every club in the bag and, if you can hold it together through the tough opening five holes, you may post a good score.

Delamere Forest Golf Club

Tandridge

TANDRIDGE GOLF CLUB
Oxted, Surrey, RH8 9NQ
Telephone: +44 (0) 1883 712274
Website: www.tandridgegolfclub.com
Architect: Harry Colt
Visitors: Welcome Mon, Wed, Thu – contact in advance

Average Reviewers' Score

Reviewers' Comments

Tandridge is a wonderful golf course... One of the more pleasant parkland courses you could wish to find... Great variety of holes with no two holes alike and tests all aspects of the game... A generally flat front 9 gives way to a generally hilly back 9 providing stunning views over the North Downs... Harry Colt echelon bunkers with those famous curling lips are present... Very good bunkering, excellent views and some wonderful changes in elevation - particularly the back nine... Pièce de résistance is the 210-yard 13th, a real card wrecker if ever there was one... 14th is worth a mention along with the 17th too – the former being the hole that is impossible to forget... Significant work appears to have been undertaken around the course recently, however it retains its character and charm... You need to be on your game to score well... One of the finest courses in the SE of England... The food is traditional and superb! The carvery – wow! This is fine fare.

Michael Holmam

ındridge is billed as "the best kept golfing secret in Surrey" but we make no ɔology for letting the cat out of the bag.

ındridge Golf Club was founded back in 1924 and the genius architect Harry olt designed the course. Today's layout is still clearly a Colt classic with onderful, steep-faced bunkering, raised plateaux greens and visionary use of the atural terrain. However, only one third of Colt's original 300 bunkers remain play. "Two new Kentish courses deserve a word," wrote Bernard Darwin in he Golf Courses of Great Britain. "One is Tandridge, which, I know, holds a high ace in the affections of its creator, Mr. olt. Here, besides pretty views, are ɔod turf, sharp sand, a bold country ıat is not too tiring and some very ɔod holes."

he 21st century Tandridge measures 277 yards from the back tees and ar is set at 70. It's by no means a ıampionship test, but it's a sporting ɔurse for the low handicapper and minently playable for the average player. he layout weaves through extensive ıature woodland where some 45 ɔecies of trees add a visual treat and enty of definition to the holes. Through ıe gaps in the trees and from the higher round, spectacular views of the North owns and the rolling Kent and Sussex ɔuntryside unfold. Tandridge genuinely as pretty as a picture.

Chris Evans – P.G.A Professional writes:
My first visit to Tandridge was on a Society day with some old friends. During the round I wondered to myself how this quite obviously "special place" had eluded me for so long. This was to change as I was subsequently invited to become the club's professional and my love affair with this classic Colt example blossomed.

The strategic layout and cunning design is matched by its grace and charm, providing stunning views of the North Downs and surrounding countryside. The rolling fairways, sloping greens and tiger tees offer surfaces to compete with the very best. Tandridge is truly spectacular and a great test of golf.

ıichael Holmam

SHERWOOD FOREST GOLF CLUB
Eakring Road, Mansfield, Notts, NG18 3EW
Telephone: +44 (0) 1623 626689
Website: www.sherwoodforestgolfclub.co.uk
Architect: Harry Colt, James Braid
Visitors: Contact in advance

Average Reviewers' Score

Reviewers' Comments

This has to be the most underrated course in the country... Simply one of the finest in the Midlands... It really is a hidden gem... From the fairly gentle opening hole, this cours proved a treat... It wasn't until the back 9 where the course really bared it's teeth with brutal stretch of four par 4s of over 400 yards each which rapidly reduced my scorecard to rubble... Greens are truly outstanding, and although the fairways are reasonably generous heather, gorse and trees await any errors... I have never played another cours with better greens... There are two other great courses within a few miles (Coxmoor & Hollinwell). However, after playing all three, I believe as a test of golf Sherwood Forest shines brightest... Sheer quality of the course and the friendliness of the members make it well worth the money... Vastly underrated... Definitely worth playing.

he royal hunting Forest of Sherwood in middle England is world famous as the gendary home of Robin Hood and his Merry Men. Sherwood Forest is also an nportant home to some of Europe's finest trees and heathland. The Sherwood orest Golf Club is now designated as a Site of Special Scientific Interest because contains the largest area of low-lying heathland in the Midlands.

ut it wasn't always this way. Life began in 1895 as the Mansfield Golf Club on the elds of Ravensdale – the area is now a housing estate. In 1911, the club became ne Sherwood Forest Golf Club in readiness for a move to new heathland ground Eakring Road. It's unclear who originally designed the new course, but we do now that Harry Colt gave his blessing to the early design. James Braid, the great evisionist, was brought in to update the course in the mid 1920s and today's yout bears his hallmark. Further minor changes – larger greens and new tees were implemented in the early 1980s after recommendations made by Cotton, ennink, Steel and Hawtree.

oday's course looks very different to the original layout, but only because ne trees have grown up over the years, creating an enclosed feeling. The back ne wends its way, each hole in isolation, through the trees. The first few holes ossess a more open, heathland feel. But there's no doubt that Sherwood Forest set on superb golfing terrain and it's also a supreme test of golf. The club has ayed host to Open Championship Regional Qualifying and even Gary Nicklaus, on of the great Jack, failed to qualify here, not only once, but twice.

enowned for its fantastic greens and friendly welcome, Sherwood Forest is ertainly a course to put on your itinerary when visiting the Midlands. Include alongside Notts and Lindrick and you will have played three of the best inland ourses in the country.

n Hall

Forest of Arden (Arden)

MARRIOTT FOREST OF ARDEN HOTEL & COUNTRY CLUB ***Average Reviewers' Score***

Maxstoke Lane, Meriden, Warwickshire, CV7 7HR
Telephone: +44 (0) 1676 522335
Website: www.marriott.co.uk
Architect: Donald Steel
Visitors: Welcome - book in advance

Reviewers' Comments

A well-crafted course laid through a landscape of woodland with ferns and ageing oak trees... Holes are technically challenging and enjoyable... After a very weak start this course just gets better and better... Course was in excellent condition for our visit eve though the weather had been pretty wet for a few days beforehand... Played in May 06 with most courses struggling for condition and it was in fantastic shape... Par 5s are good testing risk reward holes and the par 3s make you think... 9th hole has to be one of the hardest driving holes in golf... Good test of golf with long irons needed as much as wedges... It's a good golf course but not outstanding... I am a member at The Londo Club and I think the Arden is ten times better... Hotel is comfortable and provides goo facilities if you are planning on staying... With a bar overlooking the 18th the atmospher was good, if a little corporate... Thoroughly enjoyable and well worth a visit.

unded in 1970 and designed by Donald Steel, the Arden course is a regular ropean Tour venue and has hosted the British Masters and the English Open. espite the fact that the Arden is a modern course, Steel has blended the layout ely into the natural landscape and the challenge is significant, especially from e back tees – 7,134 yards. But even from the regular yellow tees, the course easures a healthy 6,500 yards.

pening gently with two short par fours, it's not long before the Arden's real st begins. The sequence of holes from e 6th through to the 9th is superb. e 8th is a wonderful short par three, ere the green is guarded by water two sides. The back nine is the most emorable, not only for the ancient oak ees, but also for the closing two holes, ich are technically excellent and very citing. The 17th is a par five where unker to the left and a lake to the ht jealously guard the green. Only the ispest of approach shots will find the tting surface. Beware of the closing le. It's an intimidating par three, quiring a 200-yard carry across a lake!

s always delightful to play a ampionship course of the pedigree of e Forest of Arden, but it's especially easing when the service and the cilities are this good.

Iain Burns – Golf Director

In the Heart of England lies the Arden Championship Course, designed by Donald Steel. It's set in 10,000 acres of Warwickshire parkland featuring ancient woodland and natural lakes of the Packington Estate. Many varieties of wildlife can be found within the boundaries of the course, providing the perfect backdrop to this championship parkland layout, long regarded as one of the finest in the country.

A variety of different tee boxes, water hazards, trees – which neatly outline the fairways – and thick rough make the Arden Course long and tough but still a very enjoyable test of golf. Host to the following European Tour events: English Open: 1993-1996 and 2000-2002 and the British Masters: 1997-1998 and 2003-2005.

NORTH HANTS GOLF CLUB
Minley Road, Fleet, Hampshire, GU51 1RF
Telephone: +44 (0) 1252 616443
Website: www.northhantsgolf.co.uk
Architect: James Braid, Harry Colt, Tom Simpson and Donald Steel
Visitors: Welcome during the week, contact in advance

Average Reviewers' Scor

Reviewers' Comments

This is real gem… Suffers from being on the edge of such a great stretch of heathland with some more illustrious near neighbours… North Hants is very similar to some of its nearby Surrey heathland neighbours – but in my mind is better than most of them… Wedged between the motorway and the rail line, its undesirable location is misleading; the course is remarkably detached from the surrounding area and boasts a number of excellent holes against a sylvan backdrop… Old-fashioned course with a balance of risk and reward holes; great two-shot par 4s, two longish par 3s with a couple of great short par 3s thrown in… Requires a tactical approach as it's testing and in mid-summer is mo akin to a fast-running classic links… 3rd, 8th and 14th are my favourites but the whole way you see quality golf holes around every corner… New clubhouse is a bit of a brute but the course is a gem! Play it before too many people get to know about this tree-line delight.

Paul Stevers

ɔrth Hants Golf Club is located at Fleet on the western edge of the glorious nd belt, which cuts through Surrey, Berkshire and Hampshire. This delightful athland course is set enchantingly amongst stately pines and silver birch trees d, naturally, heather and gorse abound.

though North Hants is not the longest course, it does represent a real allenge. Accuracy from the tee is an essential ingredient because most holes e set between avenues of trees and you'll need to find the correct part of the rway to attack the generous but well-otected greens with your approach ot.

ɔrth Hants was used for Final ualifying for the 2004 Women's itish Open and the club also stages annual amateur competition called e Hampshire Hog. Michael Bonallack ɔn the inaugural 1957 event, but failed defend his title the following year. 22 ars later, in 1979, Bonallack returned reclaim the title. Sandy Lyle and ɔrdon Brand Jnr. have also emerged subsequent "Hog" winners.

ɔrth Hants has a fascinating history t it would be remiss of us not to ention the club's most famous son ustin Rose. In 1995, at the tender age 14, he won the Hampshire Hog with ecord score of 134.

Steve Porter – Professional writes:
North Hants Golf Club was founded in 1904. The original ethos was of a gentleman's club offering golf, tennis and croquet. The course was designed by James Braid, redesigned in 1913 by Harry Colt and further improved in 1930 by Tom Simpson. In 2001 Donald Steel designed three new holes and a new clubhouse was opened in 2003. The course is undergoing further additions with new bunkers and a woodland management programme now underway.

You will find the course a challenge to test the scratch and club player alike as it asks questions not only of your ball-striking but also your course management and strategy. I am sure you will have a marvellous experience when playing this little gem of a course.

NEW ZEALAND GOLF CLUB
Woodham Lane, Addlestone, Surrey, KT15 3QD
Telephone: +44 (0) 1932 345049
Website: www.nzgc.org
Architect: Tom Simpson, Samuel "Muir" Fergusson
Visitors: Contact in advance

Average Reviewers' Scor

Reviewers' Comments

A delightful, traditional and stylish course... Always a real treat to play here… They are not overly keen on visitors but the course is a dream… Surroundings are gorgeous… Don't be deceived by the length… Accuracy is the key and the heather can be punishin to anyone thinking of trying to overpower this classic Surrey heathland gem… Once yo get onto the course you are in splendid isolation – not only because the holes are well separated but also because this is such a quiet course… Requires a full array of shots and target golf this isn't… Once on the greens you will have much fun trying to read th subtle borrows and enjoy the very true roll… Great collection of par 3s with punishing heather and excellent bunkering… You WILL enjoy your game here and you WILL enjoy your lunch just as much! Traditional and hugely enjoyable… All in all a fantastic course t play – if you're not too much of an inconvenience to them!

Andy Taylor

ıe course was built on New Zealand Farm, so-called because the original vner was one of the early emigrants. Founded in 1895 and designed by Tom mpson and Samuel "Muir" Fergusson, New Zealand is high-class golf course cated within the famous Surrey heath belt.

ccording to Bernard Darwin: "New Zealand is sui generis. It does not compete ith other courses, but it sets its own standard and lives up to it. If anyone wants play a friendly game, uncrowded and unseen, to have a good lunch in pleasant ɔmpany, and get home early to London, there is no place like New Zealand."

ot a long course by today's standards, at a little over 6,000 yards, but with a wly par of 68, it represents a challenge; ‹ of the par fours are more than 400 ırds long. Needless to say, accuracy ther than distance is important from e tee. The course plays through enues of birch trees and there is enty of heather to catch the wayward ıll. Most of the holes are isolated from ıch other by the trees; it's an intimate eling and a great place to play golf with iends.

Vic Elvidge – Professional writes:
When you come through the gate there is an immediate feeling of something very special. New Zealand, though not long by modern standards, is an absolute gem, small greens, tight heather and tree-lined fairways make the golf course a real test of any golfer's abilities.

The course drains well and is in good condition all year round. In mid-May when the flowering rhododendrons are in bloom, it has a beauty that has very few equals. The two opening par fours are a tough start and the tricky par threes make it a true classic. You need great accuracy from the tee to enjoy New Zealand at its very best.

dy Taylor

WOODBRIDGE GOLF CLUB
Bromeswell Heath, Woodbridge, Suffolk, IP12 2PF
Telephone: +44 (0) 1394 382038
Website: www.woodbridgegolfclub.co.uk
Architect: James Braid, Fred Hawtree
Visitors: Welcome midweek - contact in advance

Average Reviewers' Scor

Reviewers' Comments

Woodbridge is one of the most underrated courses I've ever had the pleasure to play... It is the finest golf course to be found within a reasonable distance of my hometown of Ipswich... I've played Aldeburgh, Thorpeness and Felixstowe, but for me Woodbridge is the pick of the bunch... Woodbridge is the one with the wow factor... The club is tuck away but once found, it will never be forgotten... it may be short, but it has an SSS high than the par for a very good reason... You need your accurate driving boots on here otherwise you'll be in trouble... 3-iron from the tee for safety on certain holes is a mus to avoid drop shots caused by finding gorse bushes... Great course presentation, very natural with fast greens all played in quiet seclusion... Worth the visit just for the taste the gravity-fed Adnams in the clubhouse! I'm considering retiring to Suffolk and if so, I'd want to be a member here... Superb.

Ted Blackbrow - www.tedblackbrow.com

/oodbridge Golf Club is an attractive heathland course located a mere five inutes away from the beautiful /oodbridge market town with its quaint eorgian shops and pubs. It's a delightful ace.

The best course in Suffolk today is, I ink, an inland one, Woodbridge, though say this with diffidence and with great espect for its friendly rival, Aldeburgh, hich is likewise excellent," wrote ernard Darwin in The Golf Courses f Great Britain. "Woodbridge has verything in the world that one could esire except the sea. It has sand and acken and gorse, beautiful turf and the noothest of greens. There is a delightful eling of being on a hill-top, there is a ne big view, and there is peace and quiet nd rusticity."

leasuring 6,299 yards from the medal es, Woodbridge is not long, but the golf truly engaging. There isn't a single poor ole on the course; many are excellent, aried and entertaining. Make your core on the front nine where there are vo par fives. The back nine is a tough rospect, with four par fours measuring excess of 400 yards.

Tim Johnson – Golf Professional writes:
Founded in 1893, Woodbridge Golf Club is a perfect example of a traditional heathland course. Fairways are lined with gorse and heather whilst over the years, oak and silver birch trees have developed, providing a splendid backdrop.

Throughout the seasons colours come to life on the course, from the vivid yellows of the gorse in flower to the rich purples of the heather. If any golf course calls for you to remember Walter Hagen's plea "to stop off and smell the flowers as they go through life," then it is this one.

There are two courses at Woodbridge, the main Heath course and the 9-hole Forest. The light land provides superior conditions all year round, whilst a premium on accuracy off the tee is required on both and wayward approach shots can quickly gather into the cavernous bunkers protecting most of the greens. The greens are fast and true all year round and their subtle nuances test even the best putters!

d Blackbrow - www.tedblackbrow.com

ASHRIDGE GOLF CLUB

Average Reviewers' Score

Little Gaddesden, Berkhamsted, Herts, HP4 1LY
Telephone: +44 (0) 1442 842244
Website: www.ashridgegolfclub.ltd.uk
Architect: Sir Guy Campbell, Major C.K. Hutchison, Colonel Hotchkin & Tom Simpson
Visitors: Contact in advance - not weekends or public hols

Reviewers' Comments

Ashridge is one of the most beautiful golf courses I've played and it blends nature and golf together in an agreeable manner... Delightful course, so expertly laid out to take full advantage of the terrain and superb countryside... Pretty course and very natural... Not the sternest test but it's fun and sheer enjoyment for the average golfer and low ma alike... No one hole stands out more than the rest because they are all of such a high standard... Lovely selection of par threes are eclipsed by the short par four 9th which is peerless... Trees are predominant and will quickly result in a dropped shot... Each time I've played, deer have been roaming the fairways. They seem very brave, especially when I'm standing on the tee! Natural quality all around... As pretty as a picture and is best experienced in late spring when the rhododendrons are in full bloom. Setting is quite simply gorgeous... Clubhouse is lovely... We were given a warm welcome.

ɔunded in 1932, Ashridge was originally designed by Sir Guy Campbell, Major C Hutchison and Woodhall Spa's Colonel Hotchkin. Around 1939, Tom Simpson ıade a few minor but significant changes. These architects made perfect use f the gently undulating land and inherent natural beauty. The great Sir Henry otton was club pro in the late thirties and during his time at Ashridge, he won ıe 1937 Open at Carnoustie. Alex Hay was also another famous Ashridge pro, aying here for twelve years from 1964.

ar 3s are very strong, with prominent bunkering providing clear definition from ıe tees. There is a noticeable split etween the front and back nine (par 5 & par 37) and the inward nine plays gnificantly harder than the shorter par 5 outward nine. Accuracy, rather than ıngth from the tee, especially at the ırn, will be rewarded and mistakes will ıvariably be punished. At first glance, ıe greens appear fairly flat, but do ot be fooled as there are many subtle orrows, leaving you questioning your yesight.

here are three starting points (1st, 10th nd 13th) all within 50 yards of each ther, close to the new clubhouse. These ɔops of holes make up the "clover leaf" ıaped layout of the course and provide number of options for players not ɾanting to play a full round.

Peter Cherry – Head Professional writes:
Whether visiting Ashridge for the first time or returning once again, golfers are always taken aback by the beautiful and tranquil setting of Ashridge Golf Club. Set amongst the trees of the National Trust Park, with the deer crossing your path from time to time, the fairways are wide enough to ensure it is not overly intimidating, but also tight enough to keep you on your toes.

The course has recently been lengthened and whilst the par fives are relatively straightforward, there are several testing par fours still lying in wait. There are so many beautiful holes it is hard to pick a favourite but the par three 11th hole, at 166 yards, is a beautiful, yet deceptively difficult test.

LITTLESTONE GOLF CLUB
St Andrews Road, Littlestone, New Romney, Kent, TN28 8RB
Telephone: +44 (0) 1797 363355
Website: www.littlestonegolfclub.org.uk
Architect: Laidlaw Purves, James Braid
Visitors: Contact in advance - after 3pm at weekends

Average Reviewers' Score

Reviewers' Comments

If you enjoy links golf, you will love Littlestone... Has none of the rolling dune dramas of the first two thirds of Sandwich or indeed Deal, just soft undulating dunes running along the coastline... Although on somewhat flat ground, the course is a pure links with the holes cleverly draped over the dunes... It's not a difficult course but it is an interesting course despite its relative flatness... Greens are some of the best in the UK... Has great greens and it's a great club but the overall course itself is not in the great league... An excellent test of golf from start to finish... Difficulty lies mainly in the bunkering... Last four holes are especially tough... 16th is a gem... Location on the Romney Marshes is peaceful and tranquil – go to Littlestone to get away from it all... Wonderful clubhouse from the old school, wooden floors, leather armchairs, a faint musty smell and a resolute 19th century feel... A joyous links course.

Rachelle Baxter

ounded in 1888, Littlestone Golf Club is a classic remote links course, located n the fringe of the Romney Marshes, with the English Channel as the backdrop. he British Ladies' Open was held at Littlestone six years after the course pened. It was originally designed by Laidlaw Purves, tweaked by James Braid at ne turn of the 20th century and modernised in the 1920s by Alister MacKenzie. rank Pennink made some bunker modifications after the Second World War and onald Steel and Peter Alliss advised on some minor changes in 2000.

ittlestone is a hidden gem, overshadowed by the other famous links courses the area: Rye, Royal St George's and Royal Cinque Ports. The course plays cross fairly flat links land, although it does have its own range of sand dunes. lew Romney is one of the driest places in the British Isles; consequently you will arely need your waterproofs. The dry, flat ground makes for some interesting ght lies but rarely will you be faced with awkward stances. The greens are true nd fast, making it difficult to hold the ball.

here are no tricks, with everything clearly in view from the tees (including a gnificant number of bunkers). You will eed to be on top of your game to keep our score together – the last three oles are amongst the toughest around.

t Littlestone, they like to get you round in about three hours (only ngles, two-balls and foursomes are llowed), but don't let this put you off. 's a delightfully good golf course that's vell worth playing.

Bernard Darwin writes:
At the eleventh there is one of those uncomfortable tee-shots, which are so excellent. There is a canal, a nasty insidious serpentine beast of a canal, which winds its way along the left-hand side of the course, and it is our duty, in order to gain distance, to hug it as close as we dare; yet if we show ourselves the least bit too affectionate towards it, this ungrateful canal will assuredly engulf our ball to our utter destruction.

achelle Baxter

HAYLING GOLF CLUB *Average Reviewers' Score*

Links Lane, Hayling Island, Hampshire, PO11 0BX

Telephone: +44 (0) 2392 464446 **Website:** www.haylinggolf.co.uk

Architect: J. H. Taylor, Tom Simpson

Visitors: Contact in advance - handicap certificate required (not before 10.10am weekends)

Reviewers' Comments

As a links course it has it all in friendly amounts, flat links holes to start and finish, undulating dunes, some big dunes, occasional blind shots, interesting carries etc... Charming, understated and as pleasing now as it must have been 100 years ago... It's possible that the first two holes will disappoint you. However, the wonderful short par three at the 5th sparks a fine run of holes, where some testing longer par fours are mixed with several short, but treacherous holes... 11th is one of the best links par threes... The perilous 13th at 340 yards is a great example of how Hayling can tease... Prior knowledge of the layout is a distinct advantage as the landing areas from certain tee shots are not obvious... There are better links courses but it's the real thing, no question... Great historical links but they need to treasure it a little more... It's really worth the visit and is a friendly place to be... If you like traditional links courses, you'll like it here.

Kev... Murray

ayling is set upon a Site of Special Scientific Interest, on the South West eninsular of Hayling Island. To the south, there are superb, panoramic views cross the Solent to the Isle of Wight.

he golf club at Hayling was founded in 1883, and the five times Open champion H. Taylor, made major revisions in 1905 and Tom Simpson reconstructed the ourse in 1933. There are few blind shots but a number of semi-blind approach hots make club selection challenging, especially when the wind is up.

he course measures more than 6,500 yards from the back tees. It breaks you gently and then really gets going after e turn when we enter the dunes. The 1th is a gem, a stunning par three called Woolseners". It measures a lowly 150 ards but it plays towards the Solent, nd often, it's into the prevailing wind the elevated green is sited on a plateau nd is well guarded by bunkers. The 2th is a tough par four, called "Desert" presumably because it runs alongside e shore – where the green is sited gainst the dunes. The 13th takes its ame from a huge, ragged bunker, called The Widow" – the approach shot is ver a hill with the Solent once more roviding a pretty backdrop.

Ray Gadd – Professional writes:
Hayling is a true links course in every sense of the word. When you arrive at the club the beauty of the setting looking across the famous Solent waters towards the Isle of Wight immediately strikes you.

The golf course is a testimony to the influences of leading course architects J.H. Taylor and, subsequently, Tom Simpson. The holes unravel to present an increasing challenge, to match any leading UK links courses. When combined with the inevitable sea breezes it will stretch the game of all golfers, who will appreciate the nuances and variety of shots that need to be played to compile a good round.

evin Murray

Seacroft 87

SEACROFT GOLF CLUB
Drummond Road, Seacroft, Skegness, Lincolnshire, PE25 3AU
Telephone: +44 (0) 1754 763020
Website: www.seacroft-golfclub.co.uk
Architect: Willie Fernie, Sir Guy Campbell
Visitors: Welcome – contact in advance

Average Reviewers' Score

Reviewers' Comments

Seacroft is an honest undiluted test of golf… A classic links, out and back… A basic 9 out 9 back layout with a small ridge of dunes between the outward and inward holes... There's nothing frilly about this links course… Really enjoyed it – I had the wind at my back for the outward nine and scored really well – same cannot be said for the return! The finish is particularly strong as it's normally played into the breeze… There are some excellent par 3s… Challenging collection of par threes... Seacroft had superb greens – th best I have played in some time… Excellent quality putting surfaces… A members' club i the true sense of the word… Bring your 'A' game off the tee and you will love it… Well worth going out of the way to play.

Seacroft Golf Club

ore than 150 miles of coastline stretch between Seaton Carew and Hunstanton Seacroft is the very best seaside links you'll find in between.

riginally founded in 1895, Seacroft Golf Club started out in life as a nine-hole ourse and, in 1900, Willie Fernie extended it to 18 holes. Sir Guy Campbell ade alterations in the 1920s, although nine of Fernie's original holes still remain tact.

he course begins in pleasant suburbia and immediately the scene is set accurate driving is the order of the day at Seacroft. The outward nine occupies wer lying ground, a small dune ridge ins down the left and the road to ibraltar Point and out-of-bounds es threateningly to the right. The 8th ole, called "Sand Pit", epitomises the iallenge. From the back tee you have to ive bravely over the edge of the road. make matters worse, a cross bunker aits eagerly to catch your best drive.

oming home, there is a feeling of evated spaciousness, which lulls the isuspecting into a false sense of curity. Gone is the road to Gibraltar oint, instead there are acres of gorse. his is no place to open your shoulders.

acroft is certainly off the beaten track, it a visit to this amazing understated iks will certainly lift your soul.

Richard England – Club Secretary writes:
This Championship Links has been in existence since 1895 as a members' owned club and proud of it. It is a traditional links out and back layout on quite a narrow site adjacent to the Gibraltar Point Nature Reserve. Adaptation to the modern game has not spoilt the gloriously old fashioned feel to the golf, with tight, undulating and hogsback fairways and a number of blind or semi-blind shots and seventy-five bunkers. The course is a Site of Special Scientific Interest, where golf and the environment join together in harmony. There are glorious views over the Nature Reserve, the Wash and to the distant Norfolk coastline from various holes.

acroft Golf Club

IPSWICH GOLF CLUB
Purdis Heath, Bucklesham Road, Ipswich, Suffolk, IP3 8UQ
Telephone: +44 (0) 1473 728941
Website: www.ipswichgolfclub.com
Architect: James Braid
Visitors: Welcome – contact in advance

Average Reviewers' Score

Reviewers' Comments

It's quite a surprise to find a little Sunningdale on the edge of Ipswich... One of the delights of East Anglia... Purdis Heath is a real beauty, a hidden treasure if ever there was one... Course has got it all with a great selection of all types of hole and a tough test... Undulating ground makes for interesting golf and although this is not a long course, there's plenty of heather and enough trees to catch you out... Half heathland, ha woodland, the course blends into its surroundings beautifully... Gentle start then it's an up, down, left, right delight for the whole round... There are some great holes, two lovel par 3s, one on each nine, and a very unusual par 4 which drops down from the fairway some 50 feet onto a sheltered green... 15th is a beautiful par 3 over water and sums up the entire course... Food is good and the staff are very welcoming... 9-hole course is good fun too... Play it and weep with joy.

swich Golf Club at Purdis Heath is a delightful place, oozing style, peacefulness d tranquillity. You would never believe you are just a couple of miles outside e busy town centre. In fact, you could easily assume that you're at one of ırrey's best sand belt courses.

ne club was originally founded in 1895 and in those days the members played n Rushmere Heath – a delightful spot – now the home of Rushmere Golf Club. 1926, they decided to move and acquired more than 200 acres of ideal golfing nd. In a similar way to Muirfield, Ipswich is laid out in two broad loops but e difference is that the loops run in different directions to those at Muirfield. ere at Ipswich – the outward nine is on the inside running anticlockwise and e inward nine wraps around the outside running in a clockwise direction. This assic design ensures that the elements hit you from all directions. Additionally, raid made full use of the natural contours of the land by laying the course out n the high ground around two lakes.

ndoubtedly Ipswich is a first class golf course, which changes character easonally. The autumn colours are sensational and in spring, with the nododendrons in full bloom, there's no etter place to be. There are many fine oles, but one of our favourites is the narming 15th, a short par three where ne tee shot must carry across water to green, which is savagely protected by unkers and flanked by trees on both des.

Ve think Purdis Heath is one of the est, and certainly one of the most nderrated courses in the land.

Sir Henry Cotton writes:
James Braid designed this course and in 1928, at the age of twenty-one, I joined Braid with J. H. Taylor and Abe Mitchell at the opening of the course and clubhouse. The clubhouse was built as a large country house so that in case the golf project did not succeed, the property could easily be sold – such was the uncertainty about the growth of golf when I came into the game!

olin Jones

COPT HEATH GOLF CLUB
1220 Warwick Road, Knowle, Solihull, West Midlands, B93 9LN
Telephone: +44 (0) 1564 772650
Website: www.coptheathgolf.co.uk
Architect: Harry Vardon and Harry Colt
Visitors: Welcome – contact in advance

Average Reviewers' Scor

Reviewers' Comments

One of the best courses in the West Midlands... Fantastic Colt design with over 90 bunkers... Excellent sandy subsoil creates an enviably good quality of turf throughout the year... Played this course in heavy rain and besides a few wet greens the drainage was pretty good... Tight entrances to greens with some subtle elevation changes make this relatively flat course a good test of scoring... Fantastic layout featuring classic Colt bunkering making accuracy a must... Make sure your bunker play is sharp – this is a well bunkered course! All in all very pleasant, nothing too demanding or spectacular... Two classic par 5s in the 7th and 15th... Par 3 13th is one of Colt's best... Host every April t the McEvoy Trophy... Always a delight to play.

David Morgan - FGA Ltd

1907, two of greatest names
' the day, Vardon and Colt, got
gether to design the classic
rkland layout that was to
come known as Copt Heath.
ne partnership of the two Harrys
as a great piece of work, bringing
mmense pleasure to thousands of
lfers. Colt's main contribution
as the superb bunkering – there
'e 101 in total – and they still
use concern to the golfer of
day.

lthough only a medium length
ourse, Copt Heath is a serious
st. So much so that the course
regularly used for Open
hampionship Qualifying. Several
claimed amateur events have
een staged at Copt Heath. The
nglish Seniors and the Champion
lub Competition are two, but the
vent that gains annual national
terest is the Peter McEvoy Trophy.
his takes place over 72 holes and
open to the very best juniors
the country. Previous winners
clude Brian Davis, Justin Rose and
ee Westwood.

Brian Barton – Professional writes:
Copt Heath is in every way a traditional golf course; it's a challenging test for the accomplished player and an enjoyable course for all standards of golfers. At 6,500 yards, not long by modern standards, but it has hosted many national and local professional and amateur tournaments, including the area qualifying round for the Open Championship. We also host our own Junior Tournament, the Peter McEvoy Trophy, which is one of the country's leading junior events.

A heathland course, reasonably flat, and easy-going on the feet, makes for a very enjoyable day out. The course has undergone subtle changes to bring it in line with the modern advances in equipment technology and is usually presented in excellent condition, with its bunkers as the main feature.

The start to the course is very challenging; with two long par fours followed by a long par three. My favourite hole is the 17th, not long by any standards, but a thinking hole. It should be possible to finish with two birdies, but this is very rarely achieved. Visitors from recognised clubs in possession of an official handicap are always welcome, but a phone call is needed to check tee availability, particularly this year, as the club has a very busy playing schedule due to its centenary celebrations.

avid Morgan - FGA Ltd

EAST SUSSEX NATIONAL GOLF RESORT & SPA
Little Horsted, Uckfield, East Sussex, TN22 5ES
Telephone: +44 (0) 1825 880088
Website: www.eastsussexnational.co.uk
Architect: Bob Cupp
Visitors: Contact in advance

Average Reviewers' Score

Reviewers' Comments

A very, very good course filled with card-less pros keeping their game in shape... Experience overall is top-notch... Quite an American feel to it, with brilliant service... The course is long with generous fairways and large sloping greens, which can be tricky to read... A big hitters' and shot-carver's delight... It can be a bit of a slog for higher handicappers off the blue or gold tees (stick to the whites) but everyone will love the range and variety of holes and the unique experience of playing an American-style course in the south of England... Is fairly open so you can give it a rip... Tremendous service undoubtedly, but the well manicured course is nothing special... Testing long layout for the big hitters, greens were true, people friendly, food good, what more could you ask for? Everything about this serious golfers' complex screams professionalism... Excellent value and very friendly.

Kevin Murray

ordon Brand Jnr. and David Gilford won the European Open here in 1993 and 994 respectively. It will therefore come as no surprise to hear that East Sussex ational's East course is a big tournament layout.

ob Cupp designed the course, using bent grass from green to tee. In 1990, after vo years in the making, it opened for play. The East is laid out in an American, adium-style design – no surprise, because Cupp is American. The earth ertainly moved here, because huge mounds flank many of the holes – making eal vantage points for thousands of spectators. The layout wends its way across e rolling, undulating hills of the South Downs.

upp has designed a cracking course that will test every level of golfer. The huge ast course measures more than 7,100 yards from the back tees. But don't be sillusioned; there are numerous forward tees to choose from. There are many esting holes and memorable ones too. But without a shadow of doubt, the pièce e résistance is the 17th, a 450-yard par four. From the tee, everything is laid out early in front of you – it's a daunting prospect. There's a wily creek lying to the ght of the green. It widens and narrows and widens again, almost reaching back the tee. At all costs, the tee-shot must avoid the creek, leaving an approach cross the water to a large, receptive and inviting green.

he whole East Sussex National complex is massive, from the car park and ubhouse, to the two excellent courses (East and West). In the British Isles, e level of customer service at East Sussex National is second to none. They ertainly know how to look after you – your clubs will be cleaner at the end of e day than at the start.

Ve thoroughly recommend a day playing the East and the West. It will be tiring but well worth the effort. Take the pressure off and treat yourself to a buggy or the afternoon round.

evin Murray

SHERINGHAM GOLF CLUB
Sheringham, Norfolk, NR26 8HG
Telephone: +44 (0) 1263 823488
Website: www.sheringhamgolfclub.co.uk
Architect: Tom Dunn
Visitors: Contact in advance - restricted at weekends

Average Reviewers' Score

Reviewers' Comments

Ah, Sheringham! A lovely course with super sea views and some testing 400-yard plus par fours… Great views as you play holes 3 through 7 along the cliffs… The view from the 5th tee – WOW! A few outstanding holes with the 5th being the best… The par of 70 safely puts the course in the 'tough' category and the SSS is higher than par – another sign of toughness… Don't come here expecting to play a classic links, this cliff-top course has park-like turf and when we played here last weekend the greens were receptive and were holding the ball well… A couple of blind drives… Good par threes… Bunkering is bold and prominent… Trains still run regularly and this makes Sheringham even more special… Your golfing experience will be charmingly traditional and dated but timeless… Spending time along this coast with the regular hoot from the steam train is certainly very relaxing… Clubhouse atmosphere is traditional but not stuffy – everyone is friendly… Well worth playing.

ıeringham is located high on the clifftops on an undulating thin sliver of land, hich is wedged between the North Sea cliff edge and the North Norfolk ailway. Steam trains and vintage diesels occasionally rattle past the course, hich is set within an Area of Outstanding Natural Beauty. The club was originally unded in 1891 and Tom Dunn laid down nine holes, returning in 1898 to extend ıe course to its present 18 holes.

At Sheringham we shall be called upon to do only a moderate amount of imbing and some of the very stoutest hitting with the brassey that there has ver been required of us," wrote Bernard Darwin in his 1910 book, The Golf ourses of the British Isles. "The theory of the good length hole has been carried lmost to its ultimate limit." The course measures 6,456 yards from the back tees, ıctor in the North Sea winds and you've got a serious test of golf. It's almost nimaginable how difficult this course must have been in the days of the hickory ıaft and the gutty ball.

he best holes are undoubtedly those that run close to the edge of the cliffs. The th "is a very attractive hole," wrote Darwin, "with the most glorious tee-shot om a high hill, a fine view of the sea, nd a fascinating approach shot at the nd." Around the turn, the gorse and ıe railway line becomes the most ignificant hazards, which wait with atience to catch anything struck ffline.

lay Sheringham alongside its near eighbour, Royal Cromer, and you'll ave played two of England's finest liff-top courses.

James W. Finegan writes:
Spotted with patches of gorse and an occasional tree, the land ranges from rolling to hilly. It is replete with natural sites for greens and tees, it is home to bedevilling breezes, and it is blessed, at 200 feet above the sea, with heartstopping 360-degree panoramas of yellow sandstone cliffs, tawny beaches, the town of Sheringham, the farms, and the wooded hills.

Brocket Hall (Melbourne)

BROCKET HALL GOLF CLUB
Welwyn Garden City, Herts, AL8 7XG
Telephone: +44 (0) 1707 335241
Website: www.brocket-hall.co.uk
Architect: Peter Alliss & Clive Clark
Visitors: Member's guests only – some packages available

Average Reviewers' Score

Reviewers' Comments

What I like most about the Melbourne course is the variety and quality... Has a touch of The Wisley, a hint of Hanbury Manor and a bit of the Buckinghamshire all rolled into one... Lethal water carries will intimidate the faint-hearted and the greens will find out all but the best putters... If you're afraid of water, you'll hate the starting holes here... Par 3 2nd requires a 190-yard carry across the river – and you have to avoid the trees protecting the green... Continually asks questions of your game... One of Alliss's better designs... As a design it's good, not great... It's a much better set-up than Moor Park... Excellent mixture of undulating greens of differing sizes gets you really thinking... 18th is one of the most spectacular I have played... Ferry crossing to the last green beats any approach I've seen on any final hole anywhere... The whole Brocket experience is classy but never over the top... You will definitely want to come back.

mere 20 miles north of London
ɛs the delightful Brocket Hall Golf
lub, set in 500 acres of seclusion.
rocket Hall was built in 1760 and
as once home to two British Prime
inisters and a favourite country
etreat for royalty. It's now a five
ar golf resort and both courses are
amed after the Prime Ministers who
sed to live here.

he Melbourne course was the first
ourse to be laid out in the grounds.
any people believe that this is one
f the finest designs from Peter Alliss,
BC television's voice of golf. The
yout follows the natural contours
f the undulating 18th century
arkland and the course belies its
ender age. Measuring 6,616 yards
om the back tees, with par set at
2, it's not a slog but an enjoyable
nd challenging test.

Keith Wood – Professional writes:
The Melbourne course opened in 1992 and was designed by Peter Alliss and Clive Clark. Created around the main house, the design is sympathetic to the historic landscape. The River Lea, which widens considerably through the estate, dominates five holes and offers an exciting challenge. The rest of the layout takes on a parkland feel and offers wonderful views of the estate and surrounding countryside. Strategically placed bunkers and small greens provide the challenge to every level of player testing the golfer's course management to the full.

The par 5, 18th offers the player a dramatic view of the main house and a great test to end the round. The approach shot has to successfully carry the River Lea at its widest towards a small and sloping green. You then reflect on your round with a trip on the small Brocket Ferry which transports you to the green.

The Melbourne course is one of the best winter courses I have encountered, providing excellent playing surfaces all year and it is now maturing into a wonderful golf course.

Crowborough Beacon

CROWBOROUGH BEACON GOLF CLUB
Beacon Road, Crowborough, East Sussex, TN6 1UJ
Telephone: +44 (0) 1892 661511
Website: www.cbgc.co.uk
Architect: Unknown
Visitors: Contact in advance - weekends after 2pm

Average Reviewers' Score

Reviewers' Comments

View from the clubhouse is quite stunning. In fact, stunning doesn't get there it's magnificent... A lovely hidden gem with links-like fairways in the summer and beautiful springy turf in the winter... This is a course you will love or hate. In summer the fairway are like concrete and, when you add this to tight, sloping fairways with fierce rough, this can be a frustrating course for long hitters... Lovely springy turf makes the walk a real joy... If you can keep it straight then you can do very well as, with the exception of the 18th, there's not much hitting to do... Short, straight hitters will love it. Long, crooked players will hate it... The views are worthy of the green fee alone and the club itself is warm and friendly... Bouncy fairways, very long rough and the greens were rock hard and fast... Really enjoyable golf and good fun too... It's a good course and you'll really love it ... Well worth a visit!

rowborough Beacon is an undulating heathland delight. The course is laid out n the southern slopes of the East Sussex High Weald, 800ft above sea level, fording panoramic views of the South Downs.

olf at Crowborough began modestly in 1895, with nine holes laid out simply on e Alchorne estate. In 1905, the course was extended to 18 holes. Can anyone nswer the elementary question as to who designed the course? Or perhaps we ould assign Sherlock Holmes to the case? The author of the famous novels, Sir rthur Conan Doyle, was the Club Captain of Crowborough Beacon in 1910, nd he lived close to his beloved course.

here are similarities between Crowborough and its delightful near neighbour, oyal Ashdown Forest, with spectacular views across the treetops and springy eathland turf. There are, however, bunkers at Crowborough that punctuate an therwise natural landscape.

ccuracy, rather than length, is all-important. The course measures a little over 200 yards but finding the right position n the fairways is easier said than done, nd hitting the small greens is also a hallenge.

's an enchanting, pretty golf course and so a genuine member's golf club. But ou can be assured of a warm welcome. hey will make your visit enjoyable and emorable because they have a long story of entertaining. We're sure that ou'll be captivated by the charm of rowborough Beacon.

The following passage was published in Henry Cotton's Guide to Golf In The British Isles and was written by David White who was then the club professional: "The average player considers the 7th to be the most difficult hole. Here the fairway slopes to the left into rough and gorse, and the second shot – which players usually find difficult – is blind over a road, with the green guarded by heather on the right."

ris Coates

WALLASEY GOLF CLUB
Bayswater Road, Wallasey, Merseyside, CH45 8LA
Telephone: +44 (0) 151 691 1024
Website: www.wallaseygolfclub.com
Architect: Old Tom Morris
Visitors: Welcome – contact in advance

Average Reviewers' Score

Reviewers' Comments

Considering Wallasey is right next door to Hoylake, there is a marked difference betwee the two. There are some serious dunes at Wallasey and Hoylake is as flat as a pancake... A great example of a real links course in the same mould as Burnham... Opening five holes and the closing three holes set in some super dunes with great links undulating fairways – the other holes are not bad but are set on flatter ground... Rolling hidden fairways and semi-blind greens and when the wind blows you have to play low running golf... Hardest hole was the par 5 13th back in the wind... Bring your best driving boot – miss the fairways here at your peril... Best greens I have played after St Andrews... Th clubhouse is grand and it is worth popping in to see the original paintings of Bobby Jone and Dr Stableford... This wonderful golf course will not disappoint you... Is a true gem and should be better known... It's much better than its lowly ranking.

Alex Sherratt

'allasey is situated on the cusp of the Wirral Peninsula with views across the ver Mersey. It's here, on the Wirral, that we start (or end) our journey after aying a host of classic links courses along England's magical northwest coastline.

ld Tom Morris originally designed the course in 1891, but Wallasey was put on e map by one of its members, Dr Frank Stableford. Irked by his rising handicap, developed the Stableford scoring system following a discussion with Duncan ylor whilst walking down the 2nd fairway. In 1932, a competition at Wallasey ok place utilising his new-fangled scoring system – the rest is simply a blob in story!

ıe opening five holes are engaging and immense fun, with several raised ateau greens and elevated tees. Long, straight driving is key to scoring well, ecause Wallasey is a lengthy challenge, easuring more than 6,500 yards from e back tees. On the surface, 6,500 rds doesn't seem long, but factor in e wind, and this will test the very best. /allasey hosted Open Championship ualifying when the Open returned Royal Liverpool in 2006, although obody was able to repeat Bobby nes's amazing feat. In 1930, Jones came rough Open Championship qualifying Wallasey and went on to win the pen at Hoylake. It was a good year for obby Jones. In 1930, he won the British ıd US Open Championships, the British ıd US Amateur Championships. After ıat, he retired. Who can blame him?

Donald Steel writes:
Long before the popular song referred to a "ferry across the Mersey", Wallasey Golf Club stood as one of the good reasons for wanting to get to the other side. Its clubhouse opposite the church overlooks the estuary; indeed, the 1st hole runs down to the point where it turns down the coast of the Wirral Peninsula.

It is a strategic position not least because it has mighty sandhills that are fascinating, picturesque and exciting, lending a thrill to the golf on some holes that would be difficult to better.

ex Sherratt

Average Reviewers' Scor

THE ROSS-ON-WYE GOLF CLUB
Gorsley, Ross-on-Wye, Herefordshire, HR9 7UT
Telephone: +44 (0) 1989 720267
Website: www.therossonwyegolfclub.co.uk
Architect: C. K. Cotton
Visitors: Welcome – contact in advance

Reviewers' Comments

What a friendly club and the course is a serious challenge, cut through miles of woodland... A great test of golf tucked away just off the M50... A true woodland cours with sweeping, undulating fairways and small greens... Tree-lined, sweeping fairways, a lot cheaper than Wentworth and Woburn but just as beautiful and testing... Many outstanding holes with a good mix of par 5s, 3s and long and short 4s... With tight tunnelled holes through the trees, you have to keep out of them otherwise it's chip out or goodbye ball but decent driving will pay dividends as this is not an overly long track... Beware; playing this course in autumn can result in lost balls, as they tend to hid underneath the myriad leaves... One of the best courses in this neck of the woods, wit top greens... Ross is special... A gem which bears comparison with the best.

Ross-on-Wye Golf Club

though the Ross-on-Wye Golf Club was founded in 1903, the club moved veral times before a densely forested tract of land became available at Jays Green the early 1960s.

n Cotton, the chosen architect, was quick to point out that the forest would be premely challenging to develop into a golf course. However, after much cajoling om committee members, he relented and prepared several possible layouts.

the summer of 1961, the lumberjacks came and started carving their way through the rest. "My first memory was the sight of the ad woodsman," wrote Donald Steel, "then his eighties, fuelling a woodland fire with sh scrub and branches and cooking a lunch bacon and eggs on the back of a carefully aned shovel." A few months later, the lldozers rolled in, clearing a path through e roots and tree stumps. After a Herculean ort, the first nine holes opened for play in 64 and the full 18-hole 6,451-yard layout ficially opened three years later.

will therefore come as no surprise that the rrent Ross-on-Wye golf course has narrow rways carved through chutes of trees, nere driving accuracy is far more important an length. Holes run in every conceivable mpass direction and it is impossible to tell nere you are in this maze-like, mature forest.

Paul Middleton – Professional writes:
Where Ross-on-Wye differs from most other courses in Britain is that it was carved through mature woodland. The tree-lined character means that it is a course of above average difficulty. There is an enormous advantage on hitting the fairways and considerable penalty for missing them, so calling for a high level of control. Positional play is essential. The greens are small and receptive if hitting from the fairway, but more challenging if hitting out of the woods. The best times to come and play are spring and autumn, when the daffodils are out and the trees are changing colour.

ss-on-Wye Golf Club

Manor House 96

MANOR HOUSE GOLF CLUB
Castle Combe, Near Bath, Wiltshire, SN14 7HR
Telephone: +44 (0) 1249 782206
Website: www.manorhousegolfclub.com
Architect: Peter Alliss and Clive Clark
Visitors: Welcome – contact in advance

Average Reviewers' Scor

Reviewers' Comments

Dramatic, varied, entertaining, exciting and exhausting sum up my feelings about the Manor House... Some really memorable holes and all set in the most beautiful hilly surrounds... Course is laid out cleverly using the land to its full effect; some of the bunkering is a bit over the top, but hats off to them for making it a visual feast... There are plenty of chances to beat par but equally many places that may catch you out (in other words, a good fair test of golf)... The incredible double-greened 17th is as dramat as any hole I have ever played. A mere flick with a wedge will see your ball rise into the air and then fall towards the green some 100 feet below... A couple of serious cardiac climbs put a slight blot on the round and I imagine that some people would have to take a buggy... I'd love to return here again to stay and play... Quality resort and a quality course through and through.

ıny people go to Castle Combe for the motor sport. It's one of the longest ablished circuits in the UK where, in 1950, a young Stirling Moss won the 2.5 e race. But the 13th century village of Castle Combe is something entirely ferent and light years away in feel and pace to the race circuit. The village is ıply gorgeous and undoubtedly one of the prettiest, most beautiful in England. fact, it was recently voted the most picturesque village by English Heritage ıgazine.

uated on the southern edge of the Cotswolds, the Manor House Hotel and ılf Club is set magnificently in 350 acres of rolling countryside. The course is elative youngster, opening for play in 1992 and Peter Alliss and Clive Clark signed it. The maturity of the setting makes the course seem much older, ıere stately oak and beech trees line the magnificent fairways. Alliss and Clark ıde the most of the undulating terrain and they've fitted the course into its roundings like a silk glove. The River Bybrook punctuates the layout bringing share of beauty and drama, especially at "Burton Brook", the 17th, one of the st and most exciting par threes you'll find anywhere.

t like the village of Castle Combe, the closing hole is one of the prettiest ishes in England. The green on this par four is guarded jealousy by numerous nkers and a series of interconnecting ponds. A par here will be a fitting end to e of the most enjoyable and exciting rounds of golf you're likely to experience the whole of England.

MANNINGS HEATH GOLF CLUB *Average Reviewers' Sco*
Hammerspond Road, Mannings Heath, Horsham, West Sussex, RH13 6PG
Telephone: +44 (0) 1403 210228
Website: www.exclusivehotels.co.uk
Architect: Unknown
Visitors: Welcome – book in advance

Reviewers' Comments

Mannings Heath is a class act from the clubhouse on... Fairways like crushed velvet and immaculate fast greens… Variety of holes is a feature, although you cannot see the bottom of the pin for your approach on the first four holes… Par 3 "Punchbowl" is as good a par3 as you could find or perhaps the trademark par 3 10th, called "Waterfall", i even better. Only you can decide… The run of three holes from 9 to 11 is fantastic (just for a moment on the 11th had a feeling of being at Augusta)… The 11th is a cracking par four and for me, the best hole on the course. "Blaster", the 14th, is a great one-shot hole… 18th is one of the finest closing holes around – take plenty of club for your approach shot across the chasm to the elevated green… There are a number of ups and downs and many of the distances can be hard to judge… Well worth playing.

Kevin Murray

annings Heath Golf Club is set in 500 acres of rolling Sussex downs and the 'aterfall is one of England's best but least well known inland courses. There are holes to enjoy at Mannings Heath, but the Waterfall is the original course and s widely considered to be the best (the second course is called the Kingfisher). ne Waterfall course dates back to 1905. We don't know who originally designed but we'd love to hear from anyone who knows.

ne 1st tee is set in the shadow of the gorgeous 17th century clubhouse and it's spectacular and daunting prospect. From the elevated tee, a long and accurate 'ive over a wooded valley is the order of the day. The 2nd is a very short par ur, but this comes too early in the round for most of us to take too much lvantage. The 5th is one of the most dramatic one-shot holes in Sussex with elevated tee shot to a green set in a most unusual punchbowl. It heralds the eginning of a fine run of holes.

easuring 6,683 yards from the tips, the Waterfall course is not the longest yout in the land but many of the holes are supremely testing and demand curacy from the tee. There is a lovely feeling of seclusion, created by the ature trees and the dramatic undulating terrain. The up and down nature of e land presents a tough walk in places and many people opt to take a buggy, pecially if 36 holes are on the agenda.

s hard to categorise the Waterfall course: it's a bit of a hybrid, a mix of eathland, downland and parkland. But this is an exciting, amusing and ntertaining course, which holds the interest all the way round.

"Mannings Heath is a great venue tucked away in stunning surroundings. I know those who visit, play either of the two great courses and sample all that the club has to offer, will come away as I do looking forward to my next visit." David Howell, British No. 1
"If there was a course I could play everyday for the rest of my life it would be Mannings Heath Waterfall course." Ewen Murray Sky Sports Commentator
For Golf Bookings Phone: +44 (0)1403 210228
Email: enquiries@manningsheath.com
www.manningsheath.com
1905
MANNINGS HEATH GOLF CLUB

BURHILL GOLF CLUB
Burwood Road, Walton on Thames, Surrey, KT12 4BL
Telephone: +44 (0) 1932 227345
Website: www.burhillgolf-club.co.uk
Architect: Willie Park
Visitors: Welcome Monday-Friday

Average Reviewers' Score

Reviewers' Comments

A lovely Surrey course that is pleasing on the eye… Nice parkland course with some really long and testing par 4s… The Old is relatively short but nevertheless a good challenge… A number of fairway bunkers are very nicely placed to gather up the slightly miscued tee shots, as I found on more than one occasion… Good greens (nice and small) for the better iron players… You need to be accurate to score well and prudent club selection is really important… I've played on two separate occasions and I've always come away impressed and had a great time… Not quite up to the standard of some of Surrey's heathland courses but from a society perspective, Burhill represents much better value and the clubhouse and facilities were truly first class… Always in immaculate condition… You'll get a very warm welcome… One of Surrey's more friendly clubs.

1907 18 holes at Burhill Golf Club were ready for play. This was a huge :hievement as Willie Park and his team had designed and built the course in st five months. The club gained enormous publicity as regular visitors included ›yalty from around the world and a collection of Dukes, Earls and Lords from ese shores. Amongst the gentry was Rupert Guinness (2nd Earl of Iveagh) and •day the Guinness family are still proud owners of the Burhill estate.

he Burhill estate is full of history and in 1940, The Ministry of Aircraft ·oduction took charge of the clubhouse. This is where Barnes Wallis set to work ıd created his legendary 'Bouncing Bomb'. Today, in and around the clubhouse, ere are many references to Wallis and his historic wartime contribution.

›day's Old course at Burhill can be described as parkland with a sprinkling f heathland for good measure. There is a great variety of mature trees and a :ather regeneration programme is now underway. The original bunkering at urhill is brilliantly strategic and even with the modern game, they still seem › be in the right place to capture any wayward shots. The greens are quite eautiful; most are fairly small but in pristine condition with the tricky slopes and ıdulations a big feature. Take heed of local advice: They all slope towards the iver Mole!

urhill seems to have slipped out of the limelight in recent years and has been vershadowed by many other great courses in Surrey. We tend to agree that urhill is set just behind some of the Surrey heathland stars, but it's not that far ehind and, with a little TLC, the gap should start to close.

BOWOOD GOLF & COUNTRY CLUB
Derry Hill, Calne, Wiltshire, SN11 9PQ
Telephone: +44 (0) 1249 822228
Website: www.bowood-golf.co.uk
Architect: Dave Thomas
Visitors: Welcome except Sat/Sun am

Average Reviewers' Score

Reviewers' Comments

Great golf course set in a superb location... From the entrance in, you know you are somewhere special... Was very impressed... Course is tough for the lower handicappe but fair for all levels... Bad shots are penalised with heavy rough which helps define the fairways... After a slow start with up and down holes at the 1st and 2nd, the par 5 3rd i in my mind the start of a great course... Topography is rolling and interesting... 8th has got to go down as one of the fun holes with a hint of quality all about it – cannot think that too many par 4s are recorded here... Holes 11, 12 and 15 reminded me of a little alpine corner seen only on ski resort postcards – fantastic... One of those places that once found, you will definitely return to... Staff are really friendly and it represents pret good value too... Promise of some onsite accommodation in 2008 can only elevate Bowood to the next level... Recommended.

:w approaches to golf clubs are as grand as the entrance to the 2,000-acre ɔwood Estate. The Golden Gates are huge and imposing, the approach road ısses through grounds landscaped by "Capability" Brown. This is quite something apparently the Black Prince used to hunt here – but what is the course like?

/ell, it's essentially laid out on flat, farmland. But don't be put off, Dave Thomas esigned Bowood, and Thomas is well-versed at subtly transforming farmland into 'eat golf courses – you may remember he co-designed the Brabazon course at ıe Belfry?

ɔwood opened for play in 1992, to much acclaim and this is a superb golf ɔurse, making best use of the estate's mature woodland. There's a fair amount f water, but rarely does it come into play because the fairways are generous. n the other hand, Bowood's length is extraordinary – measuring a monstrous 300 yards from the back tees. But Thomas thought of everything, and created ımerous teeing areas to cater for golfers of all standards.

here is a lovely feeling of peace and spaciousness at Bowood – it's definitely a ɔurse of which the members are rightly proud. The pick of the holes: the 8th – a ıge doglegged par four (stroke index 1) with an inviting downhill tee-shot, and ıe 12th – a short uphill par three with the green guarded by a stream.

ɔwood is a challenging West Country course, one of the best in Wiltshire. Play ɔwood alongside the Manor House at Castle Combe – but make sure you take ɔur best driving game along with you.

Moor Park (High)

MOOR PARK GOLF CLUB
Rickmansworth, Hertfordshire, WD3 1QN
Telephone: +44 (0) 1923 773146
Website: www.moorparkgc.co.uk
Architect: Harry Colt
Visitors: Contact in advance - not at weekends

Average Reviewers' Score

Reviewers' Comments

Moor Park defies expectations. A stunning Palladian clubhouse with disarmingly laid-bac staff... Lovely well-maintained parkland course - you'd never believe you were so close to London... The High Course off the white tees is a good test, particularly its par 4s... When you arrive at the 10th, you could be at Sunningdale or Wentworth... 8th, 13th & 14th are all fabulous holes, but the course's signature hole is the par 3 12th, a cracker. Th only minor downside in today's world is that the par 5s are all too short and can be got at by the big hitters... Lovely greens that are fair and true... Was mightily impressed wit the condition... An honest collection of golf holes... All in all a great place and don't mis a real halfway house, second only to Sunningdale in the London area... Whole facility is quality through and through, from the dazzling clubhouse with its sumptuous buffet lunc to the carvery dinner.

larry Colt designed the High course and it opened for play in 1923. Two years ıter it hosted the PGA Matchplay Championship. The Bob Hope Classic was held ere during the 1980s, along with numerous other professional tournaments. ׀ number of blue-ribbon junior events have been held on the High course, ncluding the Boys' Amateur Championship and the English Boys' Stroke Play :hampionship, formerly the Carris Trophy.

'here are some good holes on the 6,700-yard layout, opening with a friendly par our. The 2nd is a good driving hole, requiring a solid tee shot across a valley to a airway that doglegs to the right. The 4th is a long downhill par four, two accurate hots are required to reach this green in two. The 8th, 440 yards, is one of our avourites, sweeping downhill and then back uphill to a sloping green protected y a lurking pond with the half-way house sitting welcomingly behind the green.

'he homeward nine is really more of the same, some strong and long par fours vith a couple of short and reachable par fives. If anything, the back nine is more nemorable and certainly a much tougher proposition than the outward nine. Two roublesome holes are the par three 12th (one of the best inland par 3s in the ountry) requiring a bold tee shot over a valley and the 14th, a fantastic long par our where the approach shot must carry a hidden gully dissecting the fairway.

100r Park oozes quality. It's a classy golf course and a warm welcome awaits in he clubhouse mansion.

Your Top 100 Courses

The following list shows England's Top 100 courses based on reviews posted on the Top 100 website. This list is calculated on the average reviewers' score from May 2005 to Dec 2006. We can't promise it's the most definitive list in existence but it's based on the views of thousands of passionate golfers who have taken the time to write course reviews and rate each course individually.

Pos	Course
1	Woodhall Spa (Hotchkin)
2	Ganton
3	Royal Birkdale
4	Hankley Common
5	St George's Hill
6	Hillside
7	Silloth-on-Solway
8	Royal West Norfolk
9	Addington
10	Bearwood Lakes
11	St Enodoc (Church)
12	Tandridge
13	Walton Heath (Old)
14	Brocket Hall (Palmerston)
15	Hindhead
16	Saunton (East)
17	Belfry (Brabazon)
18	Royal Lytham & St Annes
19	Woburn (Duchess)
20	Worplesdon
21	Sunningdale (Old)
22	Notts
23	Swinley Forest
24	Grove
25	Moor Allerton
26	Royal Ashdown Forest (Old)
27	St Mellion (Nicklaus)
28	East Sussex National (West)
29	Moortown
30	Bamburgh Castle
31	Sherwood Forest
32	Ferndown (Old)
33	North Hants
34	Wentworth (West)
35	Royal St George's
36	West Hill
37	Chart Hills
38	Copt Heath
39	Royal Liverpool
40	Trevose (Championship)
41	Brocket Hall (Melbourne)
42	Woburn (Duke's)
43	Buckinghamshire
44	Fulford
45	Oxfordshire
46	West Sussex
47	Aldeburgh
48	Formby
49	Isle of Purbeck
50	Littlestone

Pos	Course
51	Wallasey
52	Forest of Arden (Arden)
53	Delamere Forest
54	Ross-on-Wye
55	Berkshire (Red)
56	Sunningdale (New)
57	Berkshire (Blue)
58	Luffenham Heath
59	Walton Heath (New)
60	Royal Worlington & Newmarket
61	Royal Cinque Ports
62	Woburn (Marquess)
63	Hayling
64	Prince's
65	Bovey Castle
66	East Sussex National (East)
67	Manor House
68	Blackmoor
69	London Club (Heritage)
70	New Zealand
71	Rye (Old)
72	Berwick-upon-Tweed
73	Coxmoor
74	Ipswich (Main)
75	Liphook
76	Parkstone
77	Seacroft
78	Wentworth (Edinburgh)
79	Woodbridge
80	Broadstone
81	Collingtree Park
82	London Club (International)
83	Mannings Heath (Waterfall)
84	Sheringham
85	West Lancashire
86	Burhill (Old)
87	Linden Hall
88	Stoke Park
89	Bowood G&CC
90	Cavendish
91	Mendip
92	Moor Park (High)
93	Royal North Devon
94	Seascale
95	Batchworth Park
96	Hesketh
97	Alwoodley
98	Brancepeth Castle
99	Burnham & Berrow
100	Carden Park (Nicklaus)

New Zealand Golf Club - Photograph by Andy Taylor

Manor House Golf Club

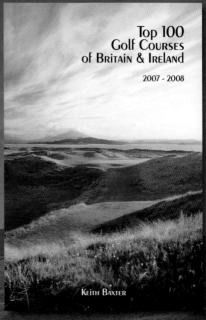

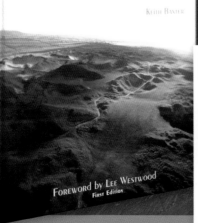

Index